W9-BZI-923

OPPOSING
VIEWPOINTS®
SERIES

# School Funding

*Lynn M. Zott, Book Editor*

**GREENHAVEN PRESS**
*A part of Gale, Cengage Learning*

GALE
CENGAGE Learning™

Detroit • New York • San Francisco • New Haven, Conn • Waterville, Maine • London

GALE
CENGAGE Learning

Elizabeth Des Chenes, *Managing Editor*

© 2012 Greenhaven Press, a part of Gale, Cengage Learning.

Gale and Greenhaven Press are registered trademarks used herein under license.

*For more information, contact:*
Greenhaven Press
27500 Drake Rd.
Farmington Hills, MI 48331-3535
Or you can visit our Internet site at gale.cengage.com

For product information and technology assistance, contact us at

Gale Customer Support, 1-800-877-4253
For permission to use material from this text or product, submit all requests online at www.cengage.com/permissions

Further permissions questions can be emailed to permissionrequest@cengage.com

Articles in Greenhaven Press anthologies are often edited for length to meet page requirements. In addition, original titles of these works are changed to clearly present the main thesis and to explicitly indicate the author's opinion. Every effort is made to ensure that Greenhaven Press accurately reflects the original intent of the authors. Every effort has been made to trace the owners of copyrighted material.

Cover image copyright Otna Ydur/Shutterstock.com.

**LIBRARY OF CONGRESS CATALOGING-IN-PUBLICATION DATA**

School funding / Lynn M. Zott, book editor.
    p. cm. -- (Opposing viewpoints)
    Includes bibliographical references and index.
    ISBN 978-0-7377-5436-0 (hardcover) -- ISBN 978-0-7377-5437-7 (pbk.)
    1. School budgets--United States. 2. Education--United States--Finance. I. Zott, Lynn M. (Lynn Marie), 1969-
    LB2830.2.S36 2011
    379.1'10973--dc22
                                                    2011008688

Printed in the United States of America
1 2 3 4 5 6 7 15 14 13 12 11

OPPOSING
VIEWPOINTS®
SERIES

# ǀ School Funding

# Other Books of Related Interest:

## Opposing Viewpoints Series

The Achievement Gap

Alternative Lending

For-Profit Education

School Reform

## At Issue Series

Are Textbooks Biased?

Book Banning

Should Character Be Taught in School?

Should Junk Food Be Sold In Schools?

Student Loans

## Current Controversies Series

Teen Pregnancy and Parenting

Teens and Privacy

The US Economy

"Congress shall make
no law . . . abridging
the freedom of speech,
or of the press."

*First Amendment to the US Constitution*

The basic foundation of our democracy is the First Amendment guarantee of freedom of expression. The Opposing Viewpoints Series is dedicated to the concept of this basic freedom and the idea that it is more important to practice it than to enshrine it.

7079655520

21.68

# Contents

## Chapter 3: How Successful Have Recent Funding Initiatives Been?

# Why Consider Opposing Viewpoints?

> "The only way in which a human being can make some approach to knowing the whole of a subject is by hearing what can be said about it by persons of every variety of opinion and studying all modes in which it can be looked at by every character of mind. No wise man ever acquired his wisdom in any mode but this."
>
> *John Stuart Mill*

In our media-intensive culture it is not difficult to find differing opinions. Thousands of newspapers and magazines and dozens of radio and television talk shows resound with differing points of view. The difficulty lies in deciding which opinion to agree with and which "experts" seem the most credible. The more inundated we become with differing opinions and claims, the more essential it is to hone critical reading and thinking skills to evaluate these ideas. Opposing Viewpoints books address this problem directly by presenting stimulating debates that can be used to enhance and teach these skills. The varied opinions contained in each book examine many different aspects of a single issue. While examining these conveniently edited opposing views, readers can develop critical thinking skills such as the ability to compare and contrast authors' credibility, facts, argumentation styles, use of persuasive techniques, and other stylistic tools. In short, the Opposing Viewpoints Series is an ideal way to attain the higher-level thinking and reading skills so essential in a culture of diverse and contradictory opinions.

In addition to providing a tool for critical thinking, Opposing Viewpoints books challenge readers to question their own strongly held opinions and assumptions. Most people form their opinions on the basis of upbringing, peer pressure, and personal, cultural, or professional bias. By reading carefully balanced opposing views, readers must directly confront new ideas as well as the opinions of those with whom they disagree. This is not to simplistically argue that everyone who reads opposing views will—or should—change his or her opinion. Instead, the series enhances readers' understanding of their own views by encouraging confrontation with opposing ideas. Careful examination of others' views can lead to the readers' understanding of the logical inconsistencies in their own opinions, perspective on why they hold an opinion, and the consideration of the possibility that their opinion requires further evaluation.

## Evaluating Other Opinions

To ensure that this type of examination occurs, Opposing Viewpoints books present all types of opinions. Prominent spokespeople on different sides of each issue as well as well-known professionals from many disciplines challenge the reader. An additional goal of the series is to provide a forum for other, less known, or even unpopular viewpoints. The opinion of an ordinary person who has had to make the decision to cut off life support from a terminally ill relative, for example, may be just as valuable and provide just as much insight as a medical ethicist's professional opinion. The editors have two additional purposes in including these less known views. One, the editors encourage readers to respect others' opinions—even when not enhanced by professional credibility. It is only by reading or listening to and objectively evaluating others' ideas that one can determine whether they are worthy of consideration. Two, the inclusion of such viewpoints encourages the important critical thinking skill of objectively evaluating an author's credentials and bias. This evaluation will illuminate an author's reasons for taking a particular stance on an issue and will aid in readers' evaluation of the author's ideas.

It is our hope that these books will give readers a deeper understanding of the issues debated and an appreciation of the complexity of even seemingly simple issues when good and honest people disagree. This awareness is particularly important in a democratic society such as ours in which people enter into public debate to determine the common good. Those with whom one disagrees should not be regarded as enemies but rather as people whose views deserve careful examination and may shed light on one's own.

Thomas Jefferson once said that "difference of opinion leads to inquiry, and inquiry to truth." Jefferson, a broadly educated man, argued that "if a nation expects to be ignorant and free . . . it expects what never was and never will be." As individuals and as a nation, it is imperative that we consider the opinions of others and examine them with skill and discernment. The Opposing Viewpoints Series is intended to help readers achieve this goal.

*David L. Bender and Bruno Leone,*
*Founders*

# Introduction

*"From journalists and educators to politicians and parents—there is a growing sense that a quiet revolution is underway in our homes and schools, classrooms and communities."*

—US Secretary of
Education Arne Duncan,
in a speech "The Quiet Revolution:
Secretary Arne Duncan's Remarks at the
National Press Club," July 27, 2010

For decades, school administrators, educators, and politicians have sought education reforms that would improve the quality of education in the United States and raise student academic achievement. One of the most popular reform ideas has been school vouchers. Issued to parents by the federal, state, or local government, school vouchers can be applied toward tuition at a private school, thereby allowing a student to have a choice of what school he or she wants to attend. For poor students with few options and a substandard local public school, vouchers offer valuable access to a better education—an opportunity that supporters of school vouchers believe could make a huge difference in a child's future. Proponents also argue that school vouchers spur competition between private schools and public schools, which will inevitably raise the quality of education offered by both private and public schools.

Opponents of school vouchers maintain that public schools should not be put in direct competition over school funding. In addition, they observe that instead of improving public education, school choice would erode the quality of schools that do not have the resources to compete with private schools. Other critics argue that it is unconstitutional for the federal government to provide money for students to attend religious institutions.

The controversy surrounding school vouchers is illuminated by the groundbreaking case of the D.C. Opportunity Scholarship Program (OSP), the first federally funded school voucher program in the United States. Developed by local Washington, D.C., educators and political leaders in 2004, the OSP was envisioned as a voucher or scholarship program that would help two thousand children from very low-income families attend private schools in Washington, D.C. Eligible families were given up to $7,500 per child toward tuition and other fees at the private school of their choice. The program had several influential champions from major both political parties, including former mayor Anthony A. Williams, former D.C. Council member Kevin P. Chavous, and former D.C. Board of Education president Peggy Cooper Cafritz. Expectations were that this federal voucher program would be a resounding success and provide a model for other such programs.

After a few years, however, there was evidence that that optimism was misplaced. The first impact study of the OSP conducted by the US Department of Education showed that there was no significant improvement of math or reading scores between students who used the scholarship to attend a private school and those who didn't receive a scholarship. Moreover, students from the worst schools in D.C. were less likely to receive a scholarship, which were assigned through a lottery. Students who did receive a scholarship had very few options for schools they could attend—and for some, the private school was not any better in quality than their previous public school.

Things worsened for the OSP when a 2007 report from the Government Accountability Office exposed the mismanagement of the Washington Scholarship Fund, a nonprofit organization that administered the OSP. Some of the private schools included in the program were unaccredited or were staffed by undereducated or inexperienced teachers. Parents were often misled as to the quality of the schools in the program, which led to children being uprooted from public schools and placed in lower-performing private schools.

Supporters of the program fired back that students who used their scholarships had a higher graduation rate than those who did not receive one. Parents were highly enthusiastic about the program. Four studies from Georgetown University and the University of Arkansas reported that they were more satisfied with their child's education, were more involved, and had learned more about their educational system and their child's needs.

When the OSP came up for reauthorization in 2009, bills were proposed in both the Senate and the House to extend the funding for the program for another five years. These bills called for a modest increase in the amount of the scholarships and a rigorous program evaluation. They also broadened the program, opening it to more low-income students.

Congressional Democrats, however, took note of the criticisms and mixed results of the program and decided to end it, which resulted in a political firestorm. With Democrats killing the reauthorization of the funding and a majority of Republicans favoring it, charges began to fly back and forth. Republican senator John Ensign, who had fought hard to keep funding, charged that Democrats were concerned more with politics than results. "In drafting this bill, Democrats put their political agenda ahead of educating our children. As a result, children who chose to leave a failing school and attend a better, safer school will have to return to the school they decided to leave," Ensign stated in a March 5, 2009, press release. "This is a tragic situation." Democrats responded by expressing concerns about the management of the program as well as the program's impact on already struggling D.C. schools.

With the Republicans winning control of the House of Representatives in 2010, supporters hoped for a chance to revive the OSP. Political leaders began pushing for renewed and expanded funding of the program, expecting better results for many D.C. schoolchildren in search of better educational opportunities.

The authors of the viewpoints presented in *Opposing Viewpoints: School Funding* discuss the funding of school vouchers and many other topics in the following chapters: What Are the Key Problems with School Funding? How Should School Funds Be Allocated? How Successful Have Recent Funding Initiatives Been? The information provided in this volume will provide insight into why school funding has aroused so much controversy, as well as the potential benefits of and drawbacks to recent funding initiatives.

# What Are the Key Problems with School Funding?

# Chapter Preface

In 2008 and 2009, the United States experienced a severe recession, which is sometimes referred to as the Great Recession. The economic downturn affected all aspects of US life. In a recession, unemployment rises, household incomes and business profits fall, and people and businesses invest less money. During this recent recession, many people lost their homes through foreclosure. Economists were worried that the recession would worsen and become a full-fledged depression, which would devastate the global economy. With the threat of a much larger crisis on the horizon, the federal government acted quickly to limit the impact of the economic downturn. Under the George W. Bush administration, Congress passed the Troubled Asset Relief Program (TARP), which provided loans to large banks and insurance companies that had made unwise financial investments and were in danger of bringing down financial markets. Loans also went to the US auto industry.

In 2009 the federal government initiated another measure to help prop up the economy and to save jobs. Known as the stimulus, the American Recovery and Reinvestment Act of 2009 was passed to help stimulate the economy by injecting funds into education, health care, and infrastructure projects. It also expanded unemployment benefits and offered federal tax incentives for businesses. Of the measure's $787 billion budget, $115 billion was earmarked for education—and it was sorely needed. Cash-strapped states and school districts were desperate for federal funds to make up for deep cuts in their state funding. Without the money, school districts would have been forced to lay off teachers and school personnel and cut much-needed programs.

US Secretary of Education Arne Duncan was tasked with managing an additional $5 billion in discretionary grants provided to states, school districts, and nonprofit organizations for school improvement. Secretary Duncan used the money to create the Race to the Top Fund, which had states compete against each other to receive significant incentive grants. He also supervised the award of $650 million in "innovation grants" that rewarded school districts and nonprofit organizations that could prove key gains in student achievement.

Funneling stimulus money into education, however, proved to be very controversial. A significant percentage of the US public was against the stimulus—some for political reasons, others for financial reasons. Some critics felt that the federal government was setting a dangerous precedent by bailing out failing schools and mediocre teachers, contending that long-term, significant reform would not happen if the government was always there to throw money indiscriminately at budget shortfalls. Opponents also argued that it was a payoff to the teachers' unions.

Supporters pointed out that without the stimulus funds, hundreds of thousands of teachers and school personnel would be laid off, programs would be cut, and students' education would suffer. For them, the federal funds were a necessary tool to ensure that the US educational system did not suffer a crippling blow at a time of economic crisis in the country and add scores of unemployed teachers to an abysmal job market.

The controversy over the stimulus funds being used for education is just one of the topics explored in the following chapter, which focuses on some of the key problems in school funding. Other topics include whether school funds are being used efficiently, the vulnerability of school funds to economic downturns, and the funding of school nutrition programs.

> *"The government's spending represents at best a missed opportunity for education reform, and a real step backward at worst."*

# School Funds Are Adequate but Are Spent Inefficiently

*Marcus A. Winters*

*Marcus A. Winters is a senior fellow at the Manhattan Institute for Policy Research. In the following viewpoint, he contends that the Obama administration's 2009 spending bill continues to subsidize inefficient education policies and eliminate cost-effective school funding initiatives such as school voucher programs. Winters argues that the administration has missed an opportunity to force public school systems to reconsider their bloated, failed policies and come up with true, comprehensive education reform.*

As you read, consider the following questions:

1. How much did the US spend on average on every public school student as of 2005, according to Winters?

2. Why does the author believe that the US government will not eliminate Head Start?

3. According to the author, why did the Obama administration's new spending bill cut the D.C. Opportunity Scholarship Program?

With two wars to fight and a reeling economy, the [Barack] Obama administration wasn't supposed to be about education policy at all. The stimulus bill, and now the omnibus spending bill before Congress [in early 2009], change that, however. The vast new resources that they shovel into public schools are sure to have an enormous and lasting impact on education. Unfortunately, though he keeps issuing encouraging sound bites, President Obama's actions so far mostly continue the Democratic Party's tired practices of subsidizing ineffective education policies and killing effective, cost-saving ones whenever they might threaten the adults who run the public schools.

## Inefficient School Funding

If there exists anywhere in America an industry begging for streamlining, it's the public school system. As of 2005, the U.S. spent an average of $10,725 per public school student. That's about twice what we spent in 1975, in real dollars. What have we gotten for this increased investment? More teachers, smaller classes—and just about identical student achievement as measured by standardized test scores and high school graduation rates. In any other sector—the auto industry, say—we would call such performance inefficient and demand that any new influx of public dollars come with changes in the way the system operates. In education, we just look for ways to spend more on the same old stuff.

During the campaign, for instance, Obama spoke frequently about increasing federal funding for early-childhood education. Count me among the cautious skeptics that such programs have lasting effects and justify the investment. Still, at least some empirical evidence suggests that starting schooling earlier benefits low-income minority students. But instead of pursuing new policies focused on real early-childhood education, the stimulus bill simply pumps another $2.9 billion into Head Start—a glorified daycare program that has no real impact on student learning, according to high-quality, government-sponsored research. A better choice would have been to junk Head Start altogether and allocate its already outsized $6.9 billion budget to newer programs that might have a chance to succeed. The only reason for not only sustaining, but expanding, Head Start is that it is an existing program that employs real adults now. The president has chosen to help this constituency rather than pursue new policies that might actually help kids.

## Subsidizing Failure

An even bigger chunk of the stimulus money—an estimated $53.6 billion—goes directly to states in the form of "stabilization" dollars tied to Title I funding and special education. As their label suggests, the purpose of these dollars is to protect states' school systems from impending cuts. New York State, for example, will get about $3 billion, which will almost completely offset the cuts that it would otherwise have had to make in the short term. While protecting against city and state spending cuts might look worthwhile on the surface, it actually represents a missed opportunity. Public school systems already have more money than they need to succeed. Severe budget cuts might have finally forced them to reconsider their failed policies. Stabilization dollars just put that off for another day. Take New York City, where Mayor Michael Bloomberg suggested that without an influx of federal dollars, budget cuts would force him to fire up to 15,000 teachers. Perhaps that would have made New Yorkers notice that union contracts' ludicrous provisions require such firings to be conducted in deference to seniority, rather than according to teacher quality. In New York, the result would have been firing nearly every teacher hired in the last three years, while keeping older teachers with bloated salaries who might not be as effective in the classroom. Such an outcome could have finally made clear how important it is to change the system. Even better, the Obama administration could have demanded that states loosen their tenure rules in exchange for the new dollars, so that any needed staff reductions could target the poorest-performing teachers. Instead, we get more federal dollars with no strings attached, again protecting the status quo and the adults it benefits.

## The Issue of School Vouchers

The tragedy is that real education reform *would* have cut costs, since the modern school-reform movement is all about adopting policies that do more with fewer dollars. The clearest example of putting adults ahead of kids, and even ahead of fiscal responsibility, is Obama's push against school vouchers. Even those who argue (incorrectly, I believe) that school choice is ineffective recognize that it is efficient. The most skeptical way that one can interpret the wide body of empirical research on private-school vouchers is that they have a small but positive impact on nearby public schools, provide at least the same quality of education to students who use them to attend a private school, and do all this for about *half* of what would have been spent if these students had remained in the public school system.

For a variety of political and practical reasons, it would be difficult for the federal government to push for something like a nationwide voucher program. However, leadership from the White House would certainly help states adopt such laws. Better or equal educational outcomes at half the price tag sounds like just the kind of program that an open-minded administration in the middle of a budget crisis should find appealing. Why, then, does the omnibus spending bill actually *cut* the little federal support for vouchers that already exists? Hidden

## Top 20 States, Per-Pupil Expenditures, 2005–06

| State | Per-pupil expenditures, adjusted for regional cost differences (2005–06) | Rank |
|---|---|---|
| Vermont | $15,139 | 1 |
| Wyoming | $14,126 | 2 |
| New Jersey | $13,238 | 3 |
| New York | $13,064 | 4 |
| Maine | $12,985 | 5 |
| Rhode Island | $12,478 | 6 |
| Alaska | $12,090 | 7 |
| Connecticut | $11,885 | 8 |
| Montana | $11,660 | 9 |
| Massachusetts | $11,545 | 10 |
| Delaware | $11,426 | 11 |
| Pennsylvania | $11,252 | 12 |
| District of Columbia | $11,193 | 13 |
| New Hampshire | $11,169 | 14 |
| West Virginia | $11,150 | 15 |
| Nebraska | $11,023 | 16 |
| North Dakota | $10,885 | 17 |
| Wisconsin | $10,529 | 18 |
| Hawaii | $10,426 | 19 |
| South Dakota | $10,223 | 20 |

TAKEN FROM: Hajime Mitani, "Per-Pupil Expenditures Approaching $10,000," edweek.org, January 21, 2009.

in the bill's sea of words is a provision that would effectively kill the only school-voucher policy funded by the federal government—the D.C. Opportunity Scholarship Program. This program offers vouchers worth a maximum of $7,500 to about

1,800 students who use them to go to area private schools—like the one that Obama's daughters now attend—instead of failing public schools that would have spent more than $20,000 to "educate" them. Cutting the D.C. voucher program serves no fiscal or educational purpose. It just does a favor for a longtime Democratic ally—the teachers' unions—whose hegemony is threatened by this and other school-choice programs across the country.

## A Missed Opportunity

Obama continues to signal, in what has already become his familiar frustrating style, that things will get better if only we wait a bit. While he is quietly killing any federal involvement in vouchers, the president has said that he intends to increase funding for charter schools. Education secretary Arne Duncan has also suggested that he will use his now-doubled discretionary budget to push increased accountability and reward states that develop the sophisticated data systems that this requires. These promises are all well and good—but it's more than a little discouraging that with the exception of an allocation in the proposed budget for a federal fund that promotes pilot teacher performance-pay programs, they remain only promises after Congress has passed a very real spending bill.

The government's spending represents at best a missed opportunity for education reform, and a real step backward at worst. Tying dollars to real reforms and taking the opportunity to cut costs by dropping failed programs could have helped improve our public schools. Instead, the president has chosen to pump more dollars into those failed programs. He says that improvement is just around the corner. How long do we need to wait?

| "Nothing moves people as quickly as the opportunity for more funding—especially in tough budget times."

# Increased School Funding Improves Student Performance and Quality of Education

*Arne Duncan*

*Arne Duncan is the US Secretary of education and former CEO of Chicago Public Schools. In the following viewpoint, he asserts that a combination of competitive and formula school funding programs (those based on students' financial need) better designed to address the challenges of education will result in better student performance and a higher quality of education for US students. Duncan outlines the investment the Barack Obama administration has made in education through the American Recovery and Reinvestment Act, particularly through competitive funding programs like Race to the Top.*

As you read, consider the following questions:

1. How much money does the author say the American Recovery and Reinvestment Act set aside for Pell grants?

Arne Duncan, "The Quiet Revolution: Secretary Arne Duncan's Remarks at the National Press Club," US Department of Education, July 27, 2010. www.ed.gov.

2. How many US students drop out of high school each year, according to Duncan?

3. Where does the United States rank in the world when it comes to the rate of college completion for 25- to 34-year-olds?

The American story is all about extraordinary people who meet the challenges of their times with determination, courage and vision. From the heroes of the American Revolution to the heroes of our transformative social movements—our nation was shaped by bold men and women who overcome resistance, fear and dissent to build alliances that advance our collective welfare.

They include great presidents, brilliant thinkers, and insightful social leaders as well as millions of ordinary Americans whose unheralded acts of generosity and courage strengthen and lift us through the everyday challenges in our communities and the national crises that test us. Throughout our history, the American spirit has yet to meet its match.

And in this ongoing American story, circumstances periodically conspire to redirect our course and lead us to a new and better place where yesterday's problems fade and tomorrow's solutions emerge with great clarity and force.

## An Education Revolution

Today, in the field of public education, this moment is upon us and I am not the first to say it. From journalists and educators to politicians and parents—there is a growing sense that a quiet revolution is underway in our homes and schools, classrooms and communities.

This quiet revolution is driven by motivated parents who want better educational options for their children. They know how important education is to succeed and compete in the global economy, they insist on the very best, and they are willing to sacrifice to make it happen.

It is driven by great educators and administrators who are challenging the defeatism and inertia that has trapped generations of children in second-rate schools. They know that every child can learn in a school culture where parents are engaged, teachers are respected and principals are empowered.

It is driven by elected officials and stakeholders outside the school system who value education enough to fund it adequately and give generously of their time, energy and resources. They know that quality education—more than ever before—is the cornerstone of a strong economy in the 21st century.

It is driven by foundations and entrepreneurs that seed the kind of fresh, new thinking that every sector of society needs in order to change and grow and improve. They are fronting real money and enlisting, smart, creative people willing to try new approaches to educating America's underserved.

## A New Approach to Education Reform

I am especially honored to be part of an administration that is playing a modest role in sparking this quiet revolution.

We arrived in Washington [D.C.] at a time when America was deeply divided over the proper federal role in education policy. No Child Left Behind [NCLB] forced some hard conversations around issues like accountability and the achievement gap but it also triggered some negative consequences.

It caused states to lower standards, mandated impractical remedies, and incentivized the wrong behavior among some educators who put standardized testing ahead of a well-rounded curriculum. Rather than driving reform at the local level, NCLB fed long-standing frustration with federal overreaching.

In February of 2009, with an economic crisis at hand, the President signed a historic law to stimulate the economy and—among other things—rescue states facing unprecedented budget cuts. The $786 billion American Recovery and Reinvestment Act included $48 billion dollars that helped save or create 400,000 jobs—most of them in education—staving off an impending catastrophe in our classrooms.

It included $17 billion for Pell grants to send more young people to college and meet a national goal of producing the highest percentage of college-educated workers by the end of the next decade. The President clearly recognizes that America must educate her way to a better economy. As he has said, "the nations that out-educate us today will out-compete us tomorrow."

Included in the Recovery Act was—by the standards of Washington—a relatively small provision authorizing the Department of Education to design and administer competitive programs aimed at improving education in four core areas of reform: standards, teachers, data and school turnarounds.

With a budget of just $5 billion dollars—less than one percent of total education spending in America—this minor provision in the Recovery Act has unleashed an avalanche of pent-up education reform activity at the state and local level.

## Setting Higher Standards

Forty-eight states voluntarily collaborated to raise the bar and create common college and career-ready standards—solving the single biggest drawback of NCLB—without a federal mandate or a federal dollar. So far, 27 states have adopted those standards. Even Massachusetts—universally viewed with the highest standards in the country—voted unanimously to adopt last week.

I want to single out Gene Wilhoit of the Chief State School Officers, Raymond Sheppach of the National Governors Association—who is not here but is represented by his policy chief Joan Wodiska—and Brenda Welburn of the State School Boards Association for their leadership on these issues.

And I also want to salute our governors and legislators for their work on Race to the Top: 46 states and the District of

Columbia brought together labor unions, school superintendents, and elected officials to compete for Race to the Top funds.

In support of those applications, 13 states altered laws to foster the growth of charter schools and 17 states reformed teacher evaluation systems by including—among other things—student achievement.

I was surprised to learn that some states had laws prohibiting the use of student achievement in teacher evaluation. Because of Race to the Top, those laws are gone.

Best of all, these bold blueprints for reform bear the signatures of many key players at the state and local level who drive change in our schools. The winners of Race to the Top will be held accountable for those commitments.

But every state that applied will benefit from this consensus-building process. Much of the federal dollars we distribute through other channels can support their plan to raise standards, improve teaching, use data more effectively to support student learning, and turn around under-performing schools. . . .

## New Programs and Grants

In the coming weeks we will . . . announce the winners of the Investing in Innovation Fund—also known as i3. We received 1,700 applications from districts and non-profit partners all across America—one of the largest responses we have ever received in the history of the U.S. Department of Education.

We will also be distributing Teacher Incentive Fund (TIF) grants for districts willing to try new compensation programs that reward excellence in the classroom or provide incentives to teach in hard-to-staff schools and subjects. The biggest single thing we can do is get great teachers into these struggling schools—whatever it takes—whether it is higher pay or other incentives.

Meanwhile, states all across America are also distributing $3.5 billion in school improvement grants (SIG) to districts that are willing to dramatically intervene in their lowest-performing schools—and to those who say this work can't be done, I invite them to visit schools like George Hall Elementary in Mobile, Alabama, and Roxbury Prep in Boston—schools that went from the bottom to the top thanks to committed leadership and dedicated staff.

Go to Urban Prep in Chicago, an all-male, all-Black high school that replaced a school where only four percent of incoming freshmen were at grade. Today, every single member of their first graduating class is heading to a four-year college; 107 students—107 graduating—and 107 going to college.

I recently talked with Don Stewart who is the former president of the Community Trust and the former president of Spelman College—and he told me that his mother wouldn't let him attend that public high school 50 years ago because it was so bad then. It took us half a century to have the courage to change and create Urban Prep. There is no excuse for that.

So there is also money for new charter schools and other innovative learning models, as well as funds for states to develop better data systems. Lastly, $350 million in Race to the Top funds are set aside for groups of states to develop new assessments.

## The Federal Role in Education Reform

All told, nearly $10 billion dollars is going out to support education reform—over and above the billions of dollars we distribute in formula grants to support low-income students and other special populations. It's been a remarkable year and a half and, among other things, I have learned much about the proper federal role in supporting education reform. It comes down to a few basic things:

The first is the bully pulpit. The President and I have both used the megaphone our position affords to challenge every-

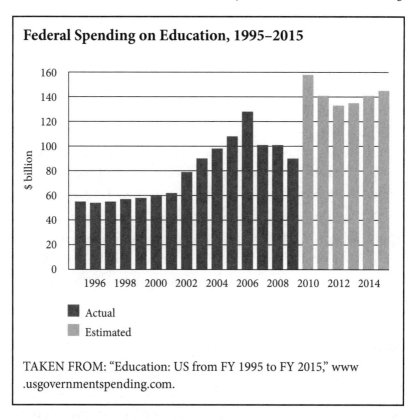

**Federal Spending on Education, 1995–2015**

TAKEN FROM: "Education: US from FY 1995 to FY 2015," www
.usgovernmentspending.com.

one in the system to get better—starting with ourselves—and
continuing with parents, students, educators, elected officials
and colleges of education.

I have been to 37 states and hundreds of schools. I have
held large and small meetings with thousands of parents,
teachers, students, and administrators. I have yet to meet one
person who is satisfied with the status quo. Everyone knows
we need to get better. I have tried to give voice to their concerns by telling the truth as I have heard it from people across
the country.

The truth is—a quarter of our students do not graduate
from high school, 1.2 million students drop out of high school
each year and there are no good options for them. That is
morally unacceptable and economically unsustainable.

The truth is—too many teachers are unprepared when they enter the classroom and the system fails to identify and reward good teachers, support those with potential or—when necessary—counsel out of the field those teachers who are just not suited for this challenging profession.

The truth is—too many schools—including many charter schools—are simply not providing students with an education that prepares them for college and careers—and they need to change the way they do business—or go out of business.

The truth is—there are indefensible inequities in our school system—in terms of funding, teacher quality, access to rigorous curriculum and student outcomes. Half a century after *Brown versus Board of Education*, this is an epic injustice for our society.

## Education As a Civil Right

We will target these schools for enforcement under civil rights laws, but it falls to elected officials, school administrators and other stakeholders across the spectrum to confront educational inequity. The achievement gap is unacceptable. Education is the civil rights issue of our generation. It is the only way to make good on the American promise of equality.

And the truth is that states with low standards are lying to children and parents—telling them they are ready for college or work when they are not. Many of those who attend college need remedial education and half of them drop out.

Overall, just 40 percent of young people earn a two-year or four-year college degree. The U.S. now ranks 10th in the world in the rate of college completion for 25- to 34-year-olds. We were first a generation ago—and we want to be first again.

That's why we ended federal subsidies for student lending programs and shifted billions of dollars into Pell grants. That's why we fixed the student loan application. It was so complicated that a lot of people just gave up. That's one more excuse we have eliminated.

We're competing with kids from around the world and the truth is we are slipping further behind. Among developed nations, our 8th grade students trail 10 other countries in science and our 15-year-olds are in the bottom quarter on math.

## Transparency and Accurate Measurements

So whatever else we do at the federal level—our first responsibility is to tell the truth—and that also gets to the second big lever of change—which is transparency. I credit NCLB for exposing America's dirty laundry [social problems that are usually hidden]—but we need to go further and show what is and is not working.

The big game-changer is to start measuring individual student growth rather than proficiency—which is in our blueprint for reauthorizing the Elementary and Secondary Act. We have to use that information to drive student instruction and accountability at every level—classroom, school, district and state.

If we know how much students are gaining, we will know which teachers and principals are succeeding—which ones need more support and help—and which ones are simply not getting the job done.

We will also know if the best teachers are distributed equitably among schools or whether the poorest kids who are furthest behind are consistently taught by the least experienced and least effective teachers.

Go to any low-performing school and I guarantee you will find less experienced teachers and high teacher turnover. Go to any high-performing school and you find the opposite: stability, experience, and a professional teaching culture.

Most states are not built to measure growth, which is why we need better assessments and data systems. We also need to look at other indicators from graduation, college enrollment and completion rates to more innovative metrics like the freshman on-track rate—which is a combination of attendance and grades—and helped me attack the dropout rate back in Chicago.

## Incentives Work

Another big lever of change is the one I mentioned before— and that is incentives like Race to the Top. Nothing moves people as quickly as the opportunity for more funding—especially in tough budget times.

When I was in Chicago, our teachers designed a program for performance pay and secured a $27 million federal grant. It would have taken us years to bargain this program with our unions, but with that grant in hand, they signed on within weeks. It was created by teachers—for teachers.

In Chicago's model—every adult in the building—teachers, clerks, janitors and cafeteria workers—all were rewarded when the school improved. It builds a sense of teamwork and gives the whole school a common mission. It can transform a school culture.

Today, there are dozens of districts with performance pay programs. There are 100 more districts competing right now for our TIF [Teacher Incentive Fund] dollars. Educators all across this country want to get better, they want results and they want the opportunity to try new approaches to learning.

So as we look at the last 18 months, it is absolutely stunning to see how much change has happened at the state and local level because of these incentive programs. That's why we're asking Congress to continue Race to the Top, i3, SIG, and TIF.

## Funding and Accountability Are Vital

And let's not get sidetracked in a false choice between competitive and formula funding—because we need both. Our blueprint and our 2011 budget request both call for fully funding formula programs like Title I [legislation to improve low-performing schools] and IDEA [Individuals with Disabilities Education Act], homeless, migrant, rural and English Language Learner programs. Even with increases in competitive funds under our proposed 2011 budget, 80% of our K–12 programs are formula programs.

Our blueprint also envisions a more humble and realistic federal role in driving reform. We are a very long way from the classroom in Washington and if we have learned one thing from NCLB it's that one-size-fits-all remedies generally don't work.

NCLB prescribed tutoring for an entire school even if only one subgroup was behind. It prescribed choice for millions of children in thousands of schools—even though there were few available options.

We want to change the accountability system in two important ways. First of all, we also want to hold states and districts—superintendents and school boards accountable. We can't put it all on schools.

We also want to stop labeling so many schools as failures. It's demoralizing and counter-productive. Instead, we want to recognize and reward high-achieving and high-growth schools—offering them the carrots and incentives that we know drive reform and progress.

For schools in the middle which face a variety of challenges, from stagnant dropout rates to achievement gaps with a particular subgroup—we will give them much more flexibility to improve. We can point them to success, but we can't mandate solutions. They have to figure that out at the local level.

The only place where we are explicitly prescriptive is with the bottom five percent of schools—those that chronically underperform year after year. We have 2,000 high schools that account for half of America's dropouts. Many of them are graduating fewer than half of their students. They're in crisis—they are denying our children an education—and we have a moral obligation to take dramatic action.

And we know what it takes: great principals and teachers and a professional learning culture where everyone takes responsibility—from parents and students to educators. We all must be held accountable for these outcomes. We have learned from NCLB that if we don't mandate real consequences in these struggling schools, nothing will change—and none of us can accept that.

## Building on Consensus

We have reached this stage of education reform after decades of trying, failing, succeeding and learning. We're building on what we know works—and doesn't work—and while there are still some honest policy disagreements among key stakeholders, there is far more consensus than people think.

Consider our system of teacher evaluation—which both frustrates teachers who feel that their good work goes unrecognized and ignore other teachers who would benefit from additional support.

Everyone agrees that teacher evaluation is broken. Ninety-nine percent of teachers are rated satisfactory and most evaluations ignore the most important measure of a teacher's success—which is how much their students have learned.

Teachers also worry that under new systems, their job security and salaries will be tied to the results of a bubble test that is largely disconnected from the material they are teaching. So let me clear: no one thinks test scores should be the only factor in teacher evaluations, and no one wants to evaluate teachers based on a single test on a single day.

But looking at student progress over the course of year, in combination with other factors like peer review and principal observation can lead to a culture shift in our schools where we finally take good teaching as seriously as the profession deserves.

## Determining What Is Needed

We also agree that the current generation of assessments don't really measure critical thinking skills and that testing only for reading and math ignores many other important subjects. Over-emphasis on tested subjects narrows the curriculum if teachers and principals believe that the only way to show student progress is to teach to the test.

But if we have better assessments that measure student growth and critical thinking skills across many subjects, we can stop assessing whether students are mastering the basics, and get a much fuller picture of student learning. The bottom line is that—if we want different results we have to do things differently.

Higher standards and better assessments are only the first step. States and districts will also need to redesign curriculum to meet those standards. And—even as districts face tight budgets—we will still need to train our teachers to help our students reach those standards.

*"Tragically, we are losing more teachers as the number of high-needs students is on the rise, with the recession creating a generation of vulnerable kids."*

# School Funding Is Vulnerable to Economic Downturns

## Jason Reece

*Jason Reece is a senior researcher at the Kirwan Institute for the Study of Race and Ethnicity at Ohio State University. In the following viewpoint, he outlines the trend of teacher layoffs and economic cutbacks by school districts across the country as a result of recent state and local budget deficits. Reece recommends more federal funding to relieve the short-term crisis and a reassessment of school funding in the long term.*

As you read, consider the following questions:

1. What percentage of school districts cut staff positions in the 2009–2010 school year, according to the author?

2. According to Arne Duncan, as cited by the author, how many teacher layoffs would result from recent state and local budget deficits?

3. How much of a budget deficit are states facing in 2010, according to Reece's citation of the Center for Budget and Policy Priorities?

Earlier this week [April 2010], facing a $53 million dollar budget deficit, the City of Cleveland's Public School district announced it would be losing nearly 10% of its entire staff, resulting in 800 layoffs and the loss of 545 teachers. Losing more than 800 staff will be devastating to a high-need district (in which 100% of students are identified as being economically disadvantaged) and which is already identified as being on "academic watch" for meeting only 3 of 30 educational standards in 2008–2009. These impending layoffs would also severely impede the district's plan to use special "innovation" schools to promote academic achievement in the district.

## A Serious National Problem

This startling headline points to a troubling trend that looks to be a growing national problem. National surveys of school administrators found that nearly 70% of districts cut staff positions in this last school year and 90% expect to have layoffs next year. Education Secretary Arne Duncan recently stated that recent state and local budget deficits would probably result in 100,000 to 300,000 teacher layoffs.

To put that figure in perspective, consider that 300,000 teaching positions represent close to 9% of the total 3.4 million K–12 teaching jobs reported for the nation in 2008 by the Bureau of Labor Statistics. Or that 300,000 public school teacher layoffs would represent half of the 608,000 jobs reported to be "supported or created" in the fourth quarter of 2009 by the nearly $780 billion dollar stimulus package.

These recent headlines are more frightening when you consider two looming financial challenges facing public schools. Most public schools derive a significant portion of tax revenue from local property taxes which are often based on property values. But, property values are not set in stone; the housing crisis has produced a drop in property values across the nation and resulted in dramatic devaluation in some markets.

## A Dwindling Tax Base

The impact on local tax base is uncertain at this time, but we can reasonably speculate that decline in home values will eventually produce a severe drain on the local tax base. States also fund a significant portion of public education and looming deficits facing state government are sure to impact public school funding in the future. The Center for Budget and Policy Priorities estimates that in 2010 states are facing $128 billion in budget deficits; another $260 billion in state budget deficits are expected to follow in 2011 and 2012.

Racial and social equity concerns are directly impacted by this challenge as it unfolds in schools across the nation. The longstanding achievement gap facing our most vulnerable and marginalized students is well documented and inequality in schools persists. Schools in the US have also rapidly re-segregated along lines of race and class, producing many schools and districts with large numbers of high-needs students and less financial resources than more affluent school districts. Tragically, we are losing more teachers as the number of high-needs students is on the rise, with the recession creating a generation of vulnerable kids, especially among communities and populations hit hardest by the recession. Instead of having more resources and skilled educators to target at this growing challenge, districts are forced to cut staff at a time of escalating need.

## A Federal Solution

What is the solution to this impending crisis? In short, we need more federal funding to relieve the immediate crisis, especially targeting our highest-need schools or school districts

## Looking to the Future of School Funding

Clearly, the current system of school funding isn't working. For schools to succeed in the long run, school boards, policymakers, and the public need to reexamine how public education is funded at the local, state, and federal levels. Federal ARRA [American Recovery and Reinvestment Act] and Education Jobs Fund are simply tourniquets for hemorrhaging local and state education budgets. We need a new system that will stop the bleeding permanently by providing reliable and sustainable funding for public education. What that new funding system looks like should be the subject of a serious national conversation—and the subject of in-depth research.

Districts need to communicate how severe the long-term outlook is and work to ensure that students who are just starting school now will be able to compete with their international peers when they graduate from high school. Asking schools to do more with less does not make sense. How much less can schools have before they are unable to do more? How much erosion in the quality of public education can the nation sustain?

Jim Hull, "Cutting to the Bone:
How the Economic Crisis Affects Schools,"
The Center for Public Education, October 7, 2010.

like Cleveland, where cuts will be the sharpest and students will be the most vulnerable. In the long term, this challenge should cause us to seriously rethink our structurally inequitable and antiquated method for funding our public schools.

We also must consider if we are adequately targeting resources to those schools with the highest needs, schools whose children are at greatest risk and schools which are often at the greatest fiscal peril. If we fail to turn this challenge into an opportunity to address these longstanding problems, we risk losing progress for not only a whole generation of kids, but also endanger our nation's ability to compete and excel in the hypercompetitive knowledge-based 21st century global economy.

| "For a variety of reasons, from one year to the next, schools almost always have more real revenue for each of their enrolled students."

# The Federal Government Protects Student Funding from Economic Downturns

*Arthur Peng and James Guthrie*

*James Guthrie is professor of public policy and education at Vanderbilt University and director of the Peabody Center for Education Policy. Arthur Peng is a research associate at the Peabody Center. In the following viewpoint, they assert that despite newspaper headlines to the contrary, there is not a school funding crisis—school districts almost always have enough revenue year after year. Guthrie and Peng outline the various factors that allow school districts to be relatively insulated from economic downturns.*

As you read, consider the following questions:

1. According to the authors, how much have teacher salaries increased over the past fifty years?

Arthur Peng and James Guthrie, "The Phony Funding Crisis," *Education Next*, Winter 2010. Copyright © 2010 by Education Next. All rights reserved. Reproduced by permission.

2. What do the authors say the federal government has done regarding school funding for the first time in history?

3. How many times has per-pupil spending declined since 1929, according to the authors?

Chicken Little is alive and seemingly employed as a finance analyst or reporter for an education interest group. If one relies on newspaper headlines for education funding information, one might conclude that America's schools suffer from a perpetual fiscal crisis, every year perched precariously on the brink of financial ruin, never knowing whether there will be sufficient funding to continue operating. Budgetary shortfalls, school district bankruptcies, teacher and administrator layoffs, hiring and salary freezes, pension system defaults, shorter school years, ever-larger classes, faculty furloughs, fewer course electives, reduced field trips, foregone or curtailed athletics, outdated textbooks, teachers having to make do with fewer supplies, cuts in school maintenance, and other tales of fiscal woe inevitably captivate the news media, particularly during the late-spring and summer budget and appropriations seasons.

Yet somehow, as the budget-planning cycle concludes and schools open their doors in the late summer and fall, virtually all classrooms have instructors, teachers receive their paychecks and use their health plans, athletic teams play, and textbooks are distributed. Regrettably, this story is seldom accorded the same media attention as are the prospects of budget reductions and teacher layoffs.

## The Real Story

For a variety of reasons, from one year to the next, schools almost always have more real revenue for each of their enrolled students. For the past hundred years, with rare and short ex-

## How Is Education So Well Protected During Recessions?

Public schools have long been remarkably insulated from economic downturns. This becomes particularly clear when we compare employment trends in different economic sectors. . . . Employment levels reflect economic conditions and, except for government (which includes elementary and secondary education), employment levels fluctuate with the economy and the historical trend is modestly upward. . . .

Unlike other employment sectors, education is protected from the direct effects of economic ups and downs by an interlocking and reciprocally reinforcing set of politically constructed conditions. Among these conditions are 1) education's privileged legal status in most state constitutions; 2) schooling's uniquely decentralized operation and diffuse revenue-generation structure; 3) local political dynamics and institutions that foster a favorable fiscal environment for public schools; 4) a multitiered structure for funding schools with complicated intergovernmental funding incentives and reliance on inelastic tax sources, such as property taxes at the local level. Almost no other economic endeavor enjoys such a spectrum of insulating conditions.

> *"Spending money as fast as it can be printed is shortsighted and meaningless without long-term improvements and accountability goals firmly attached."*

# Federal Stimulus Money Should Not Be Used for Education

## Lynne K. Varner

*Lynne K. Varner is an editorial columnist for the* Seattle Times. *In the following viewpoint, she asserts that another round of stimulus funds going to public education is counterproductive unless it comes with significant streamlining and reform. Varner argues that stimulus funds should not be allocated until teachers' unions are ready to make sensible concessions.*

As you read, consider the following questions:

1. According to Varner, how much money did Congress consider sending to public schools?

2. How much stimulus money did Congress send to schools in 2009, according to the author?

3. According to the American Association of School Administrators, as cited by the author, how many jobs might have to be cut by cash-strapped districts in 2011?

Down the road, Congress backing away from a $23 billion rescue of public schools will be remembered as a blessing disguised as political inaction.

Few among us would argue public schools do not have significant needs, including the persistent call for more robust and consistent local funding. But another round of federal stimulus—on top of the $100 billion sent to help schools just a year ago [2009]—adds way too much to mounting federal debt with too little in return.

Time to do what we wish BP [British Petroleum] would do about the oil spill in the gulf [of Mexico] and put a lid on the flow of federal stimulus.

## Funds Are Not Critical

A compelling case for deficit spending, as argued by National Economic Council Director Lawrence H. Summers recently, is if it spurs the economy and produces maximum "bang for the buck."

Under this lens, the case Congress is making for education stimulus, round two, falls apart.

While the American Association of School Administrators warns that cash-strapped districts might be forced to cut as many as 275,000 jobs for next year [2011] most school districts have already written their budgets and, by state law, had to notify teachers last month [May 2010] of layoffs next fall.

The number of layoffs are smaller, at least in this area, than expected. And budget numbers cast in a more conservative light left some wiggle room, meaning it is unlikely all of the teachers notified about layoffs will actually lose their jobs.

This doesn't mean the situation isn't still critical, but it does lack the dire urgency appropriate for deficit spending.

## The Benefits Are Unclear

Adding billions more to the federal tab our children will pay might have been easier to swallow if the benefits were clear, or even existed. But the only thing proponents of more stimulus have been able to say is that it will save teaching jobs.

Left ignored is the question of whether all of those jobs *should* be saved. A smart federal rescue would not only save jobs, it would save the jobs of the best teachers in the K–12 system. It is a mystery why the bills' sponsors, Sen. Tom Harkin, D-Iowa, and Rep. George Miller, D-Calif., didn't use the opportunity to press for layoffs based on performance rather than seniority.

More troubling news comes from a *Washington Post* editorial that points out the money would have been distributed to states based on population, not expected layoffs. "States where no layoffs are imminent would get checks anyway, and the majority of states would receive more than they could possibly need to avoid layoffs," the editorial read. Not to be outdone, the Senate version permits the excess money to be spent on other things.

C'mon lawmakers: Pork [politically motivated spending] by any other name still oinks.

## Stimulus Funding Is Not a Real Solution

The so-called rescue money would've mollified teachers unions in need of some good old political stroking after the [Barack] Obama administration's aggressive education-reform push. But the money would not have resulted in a game-changer public school parents are desperately calling for.

I want to see more money going to schools, but when every dollar counts, we can't afford money that doesn't take us farther down the road toward reform. Spending money as fast as it can be printed is shortsighted and meaningless without long-term improvements and accountability goals firmly attached.

A tough line on this is crucial. Policymakers concerned about growing income inequality will start to place even more pressure on public education as part of the solution. Compounding efforts to dramatically improve schools is an annual report by the U.S. Department of Education tracking a rise in schools segregated by poverty and race.

These trends point to problems that could easily eat up $23 billion if Congress is in such a spendy mood.

The political cover story on the education stimulus bill will be that Democrats favored it because they support schools and the Republicans who balked hate schools. Don't believe the hype. This was a thinly disguised blessing that will prove its worth to the bottom line in the months ahead.

*"Even if investing in education isn't what gets us out of this recession, it will go a long way toward preventing it from happening again."*

# Federal Stimulus Money Should Be Used for Education

## The Daily Collegian

*The* Daily Collegian *is the student-run newspaper of Pennsylvania State University. In the following viewpoint, the author contends that the school funding coming from the 2009 stimulus bill is a wise investment. The editorial argues that the money will go a long way toward generating economic growth and will give schools a chance to improve the quality of education for their students.*

As you read, consider the following questions:

1. How many billions of dollars does the author claim were spent as part of the stimulus bill passed in 2009?

2. How much of the stimulus bill was slated for education, according to the editorial?

3. What do the authors say about public school teachers' unions and the tenure system at universities?

America, prepare to be stimulated.

The House of Representatives recently [in 2009] passed an economic stimulus bill of more than $800 billion, and the Senate is expected to approve of a similar price tag with differences in the appropriations. The combined negotiated bill is expected to land on President [Barack] Obama's desk within the week.

Of this bill, approximately $150 billion is slated for education, from preschool up through the university level, including increases in federal student-aid programs, extra assistance for researchers and funding for campus infrastructure.

While there is still disagreement about the specific appropriations of the bill, with the House including $40 billion more for state and local governments, the dedication to educational spending must be maintained throughout the negotiations.

The country's economic situation is dire, and a stimulus plan needs to make an impact immediately. It will take years if not decades for the results of an investment in education to manifest itself.

Although $150 billion is a significant portion of the stimulus funds to invest long-term, it's also a wise decision.

Both versions of the bill include significant increases in funding for Pell grants, the government's primary aid program for low-income college students, and an expansion of the Hope tuition tax credit.

## A Long-Term Investment in Education

While the results won't be tangible right away, they're a very safe bet to be tangible eventually. Even if investing in education isn't what gets us out of this recession, it will go a long way toward preventing it from happening again.

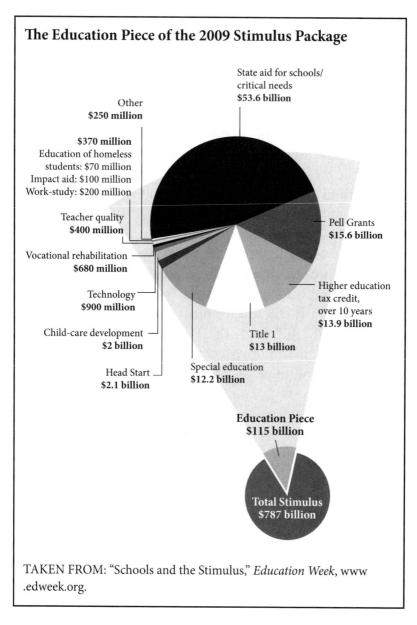

The Education Piece of the 2009 Stimulus Package

State aid for schools/critical needs **$53.6 billion**

Other **$250 million**

**$370 million**
Education of homeless students: $70 million
Impact aid: $100 million
Work-study: $200 million

Teacher quality **$400 million**

Vocational rehabilitation **$680 million**

Technology **$900 million**

Child-care development **$2 billion**

Head Start **$2.1 billion**

Pell Grants **$15.6 billion**

Higher education tax credit, over 10 years **$13.9 billion**

Title 1 **$13 billion**

Special education **$12.2 billion**

**Education Piece $115 billion**

**Total Stimulus $787 billion**

TAKEN FROM: "Schools and the Stimulus," *Education Week*, www.edweek.org.

Naturally, throwing money at something—even $150 billion—is no guarantee for success, but giving schools the means to improve certainly helps. From attracting better teachers to implementing up-to-date technology, schools need money. Badly.

Moreover, education is a fairly secure investment if only for the fact that it's an industry that cannot be outsourced, at least for the foreseeable future.

With all this in mind, $800 billion (and, in fact, $150 billion) is an awful lot of money, and as Sen. John Ensign, R-Nev., said in the *New York Times*, "You don't get do-overs with a trillion dollars." This needs to be done right.

The amount of money in play here necessitates some level of restrictions and caveats. For one thing, the unionization of public school teachers and the tenure system in place at the university level can have a calcifying effect on the education system. With the money, there must also be some attempt to hold accountable the educators currently in place. Education has proven consistently to be an efficient engine of economic growth, albeit an eventual, rather than an immediate, one. Because most of the stimulus bill will go toward generating economic growth right away, portioning off some of it for long-term cultivation is a prudent move.

# Periodical and Internet Sources Bibliography

*The following articles have been selected to supplement the diverse views presented in this chapter.*

| | |
|---|---|
| Raven Clabough | "Federal Stimulus Almost Gone: Education Budget Woes," *New American*, February 9, 2010. |
| Sam Dillon | "Stimulus Plan Would Provide a Flood of Aid to Education," *New York Times*, January 27, 2009. |
| Bob Herbert | "Unfazed by Reality," *New York Times*, June 14, 2010. |
| Erica Jacobs | "Can School Lunches Be Improved? Yes They Can!" *Washington Examiner*, August 31, 2010. |
| Lenny Klompus | "Federal Stimulus Funds Will Support Students at Schools That Do Not Meet Adequate Yearly Progress," *Hawaii Reporter*, October 28, 2010. |
| Pedro Noguera | "Obama Administration Needs to Change Direction on Education," *The Progressive*, August 5, 2010. |
| Jamie Oliver | "Schoolkids Deserve More Than Junk Food," CNN.com, October 7, 2010. |
| Paul E. Peterson | "A Recession for Schools," *Education Next*, Winter 2010. |
| Stacy L. Sobell | "School Meals: Agenda's First Course Should Be Quality and Access," OregonLive.com, August 29, 2010. |
| Linda Stone | "Congress Should Feed Hungry Kids When Need Is Greatest," *Seattle Times*, July 16, 2010. |
| Marty Walz | "The Positive Impact of the Federal Stimulus Law," wickedlocal.com, June 21, 2010. |

OPPOSING
VIEWPOINTS®
SERIES

# CHAPTER 2

# How Should School Funds Be Allocated?

# Chapter Preface

When the United States fell into a severe recession in 2008, the federal government jumped into action to help keep the economy afloat and limit the extent of the economic damage. One of the key measures initiated by the Barack Obama administration was the American Recovery and Reinvestment Act of 2009, also known as the stimulus, which injected funds into education, health care, and infrastructure projects.

On July 24, 2009, President Obama and US Department of Education Secretary Arne Duncan announced that $4.35 billion of the $115 billion earmarked for education would be set aside for a special program that was created to spur education reform. Known as Race to the Top, the program accepted applications from states that competed against each other for funds. States were evaluated on six criteria: having effective teachers who are supported with excellent resources; closing the gap between achievement standards and actual student achievement; developing and implementing common standards and assessments; having successful charter schools; turning around the lowest-achieving schools; and fully utilizing data systems to achieve superior results.

Cash-strapped states quickly took action to better their chances to win Race to the Top funds. Forty-eight states adopted common standards for K–12. Some states implemented radical reform: for example, Illinois allowed more charter schools and Massachusetts made it easier for students in lower-rated schools to switch to charter schools. In his July 27, 2010, remarks at the National Press Club, Duncan outlined the benefits:

> In support of those applications, 13 states altered laws to foster the growth of charter schools and 17 states reformed 'teacher evaluation systems by including—among other things—student achievement.

I was surprised to learn that some states had laws prohibiting the use of student achievement in teacher evaluation. Because of Race to the Top, those laws are gone.

Best of all, these bold blueprints for reform bear the signatures of many key players at the state and local level who drive change in our schools. The winners of Race to the Top will be held accountable for those commitments.

But every state that applied will benefit from this consensus-building process. Much of the federal dollars we distribute through other channels can support their plan to raise standards, improve teaching, use data more effectively to support student learning, and turn around under-performing schools.

Winners were chosen in two rounds, receiving awards ranging from $20 million to $700 million, depending on the state's share of the federal population of schoolchildren. Only the four largest US states—California, New York, Florida, and Texas—were eligible for the largest amounts.

On March 29, 2010, Tennessee and Delaware were announced as the only winners of the first round, receiving $500 million and $100 million, respectively. On August 24, 2010, the second-round winners were announced: the District of Columbia ($75 million), Florida ($700 million), Georgia ($400 million), Hawaii ($75 million), Maryland ($250 million), Massachusetts ($250 million), New York ($700 million), North Carolina ($400 million), Ohio ($400 million), and Rhode Island ($75 million).

The Race to the Top program has generated considerable controversy. Many state politicians and teachers' unions resented the interference of the federal government in school reform and school funding. Texas, for example, declined to participate in the program. As Texas governor Rick Perry announced in a January 13, 2010, press release, "Texas is on the right path toward improved education, and we would be foolish and irresponsible to place our children's future in the hands of unelected bureaucrats and special interest groups thousands of miles away in Washington [D.C.], virtually eliminating parents' participation in their children's education. If Washington were truly concerned about funding education with solutions that match local challenges, they would make the money available to states with no strings attached." Other critics argued that the reforms required by Race to the Top had been unsuccessful in the past, and opponents detected an East Coast, urban bias to the awards.

The effectiveness of the Race to the Top program is one of the topics explored in the following chapter, which focuses on how school funds should be allocated. Other subjects in the chapter include the use of weighted student funding allocations, the 65 percent funding strategy, and the wisdom of tying national standards to federal school funding.

> "Creating a Weighted Student Funding formula forces a school system to re-examine where it spends its dollars, and the outcomes it produces in student learning."

# Weighted Student Funding Effectively Allocates Resources

## Christian Braunlich

*Christian Braunlich is vice president of the Thomas Jefferson Institute for Public Policy, a nonpartisan public policy foundation in Virginia. He served for eight years on the school board for Fairfax County, Virginia. In the following viewpoint, he advocates a system of weighted student funding (WSF). Under such a system, funding would be based on a student's needs and would follow a student to whatever public school he or she attends. Braunlich argues that WSF would effectively allocate resources, improve accountability, and provide autonomy and flexibility for school principals.*

As you read, consider the following questions:

1. According to the author, who first proposed a system of weighted student funding?

2. How many school districts use some form of weighted student funding, according to the author?

3. In the author's view, how does WSF smooth out budget reductions?

Beset by reduced tax revenues, school divisions across Virginia have been scrambling to balance their budgets.

But while federal stimulus funds may have provided many with a temporary reprieve, those funds won't last forever—and without having made systemic reforms that gain greater efficiencies, in a few years school systems will find themselves back where they started.

One such reform would be to establish a system of Weighted Student Funding (WSF), first proposed in 2006 by a bipartisan coalition whose members ranged from Bill Clinton's Chief of Staff to Ronald Reagan's Education Secretary.

## What Is Weighted Student Funding?

The essence of the concept was that funding, weighted according to a student's needs, should follow that child to whatever public school he or she attends, and that funding should arrive at the school as real dollars (not teaching positions, ratios or staffing). Simultaneously, the program pushes down decision-making and spending transparency to the school level, so that funds can be spent based on the needs of the kids while focusing on results.

Autonomy, flexibility and real decision-making power is made at the principal level, where the needs of the individual school and individual students are best known. Meanwhile, principals are held accountable [for] transparent outcomes to clear performance goals.

I've long argued that such an approach better meets the needs of students in a diverse world no longer populated by the cast of *Ozzie and Harriet* [a popular family TV comedy in

## Weighted Student Funding

In the United States weighted student formula-like initiatives exist in at least 14 school districts and the state of Hawaii. In addition, several other school districts and states—including Philadelphia, Ohio, New Jersey, Indiana, Louisiana, South Carolina and Delaware—have expressed interest in moving toward a weighted student formula budgeting system.

The weighted student formula is a policy tool and financing mechanism that has the potential to be implemented by governors within the confines of existing state education budgets and economic constraints to create more efficient, transparent and equitable funding. Weighted student formula is a student-driven rather than program-driven budgeting process. It goes by several names including results-based budgeting, student-based budgeting, "backpacking" or fair-student funding. In every case the meaning is the same: dollars rather than staffing positions follow students into schools. In many cases, these resources are weighted based on the individual needs of the student.

*Lisa Snell,*
*Weighted Student Formula Yearbook 2009,*
*Reason Foundation, 2009.*

the 1950s and '60s]. But until now, no one had examined the result of such funding in those few cities that had incorporated it.

## A Study of WSF

Comes now a new *Weighted Student Funding Yearbook* published by the Reason Foundation. This yearbook looks at the

15 school districts that are using some form of WSF, examining the best practices that have helped school systems eliminate funding wasted on bureaucracy and drive more dollars into schools and individual classrooms.

For example—

- Prior to 2008, less than half of Hartford, Connecticut's education funding made it to the classroom. With WSF, the district redirected resources to the schools with a 20 percent reduction in central office expenses and elimination of more than 40 district-level staff positions.

- Last year, Baltimore (MD) City Schools confronted a budget shortfall of nearly $80 million. By creating a "fair student funding plan," $165 million in cuts from the central office not only covered the shortfall but also allowed the redistribution of $88 million to the schools. By next year, the Superintendent will have cut 489 jobs from the central office, re-directing 80 percent of the district operating budget to the schools.

- WSF also smoothes out budget reductions. Under current systems, schools funded on a staffing model can lose entire teaching positions when fewer students are enrolled. But in Poudre (CO), schools lose only the funding associated with the student and have the flexibility to shift funding around to avoid dramatic staffing losses.

- And even as Oakland (CA) schools were forced to make significant budget cuts, most of those reductions took place at the central office level, while nearly 90 percent of the unrestricted funding assigned to schools continued to flow there.

Creating a Weighted Student Funding formula forces a school system to re-examine where it spends its dollars, and the outcomes it produces in student learning. In turn, that re-examination gives a school system few options other than to spend the funds where it will get the greatest returns—at the school level, not the district level.

## The Benefits of WSF

And it empowers those at the school level to decide how best to spend those monies, by relieving them of decisions made centrally. Principals decide if dollars should be spent each year on a new teacher, new books, new software or better communications with parents.

Admittedly, the school systems now using some variant of weighted student funding are all larger than most of those in Virginia. At 22,000 students, Hartford is the smallest, yet is larger than all but 12 Virginia school divisions. But those 12 school divisions educate more than half the public schoolchildren in Virginia, supported by a concomitant percentage of taxpayer dollars.

And at a time of budgetary crisis, reforming half the dollars spent is better than reforming none.

than the worst-funded schools, they also have more black students. The difference in spending is largely due to class size and school size: on average, bigger classes and bigger schools spend less money per student on instruction.

## "Need-Based" Weight

Klein could have tackled the problem by assigning each student a fixed amount of money for instructional spending, with slightly more spending for older students, and allowing the funds to follow students into whichever schools they attended. Instead, the chancellor chose to assign each student a "need-based weight" and to fund that student—really, that student's school—accordingly. Under the new formula, as the IBO report details, each school will start out with "foundation money" of $200,000; each student will then get a "base weight" allotment of roughly $4,000, with slightly more money for middle- and high-school kids. After those initial allocations, the formula gets complicated. Each student scoring "well below standards" and entering fourth or fifth grade, or a high-school grade, gets an extra $1,500; students "below standards" get more than $900. Middle-school kids scoring "well below standards" get nearly $1,900, with "below standards" kids getting an extra $1,300. And each student who enters school in poverty before the fourth grade gets an extra $900 (these younger kids haven't taken any standardized tests yet, so the education department is using poverty as a proxy for low achievement, since more than 90 percent of low-achieving students are poor, according to city data).

Special-ed students will get as much as $9,500 above the baseline annually, depending on how much of the day they spend in special instruction. "English language learners" will get $1,500 to $1,900 more than the base, and transfer students under the No Child Left Behind law will get slightly more than that. By contrast, a student at an academically competitive school like Stuyvesant—where prospective students have to take a tough entrance exam—would get only $950 above his "base weight." These changes will be gradual, partly in response to union and legislative opposition, with previously overfunded schools getting to keep their extra money for at least two years. But over time, if New York's next mayor decides to keep the program in place—certainly not a guarantee, though Democratic officials in much smaller cities have embraced similar ideas—they will have a significant effect on school funding.

## Problems with FSF

The education department designed the new funding structure so that schools won't be penalized if, say, a student scoring "well below standards" improves; the school will get to keep his money despite the improvement. But the structure certainly offers potential for fraud. Schools will have an incentive to keep borderline kids in special ed, or keep them in it for a greater portion of the school day.

More importantly, the plan formally defines the public school system as a social-service program that transfers wealth from the rich and the middle class to the poor. Political scientists know that the most efficient way to erode public support for a universal program is to turn it into a program for the poor; that's why it was much easier to reform welfare than it has been so far to reform Social Security and Medicare. And though 70 percent of public school students are poor, the system depends on middle-class support. Many middle-class residents in Brooklyn, Queens, and Staten Island send their kids to public schools, accounting for a good part of the 30 percent of students who aren't poor. These voters are among those New Yorkers who often tell pollsters that quality education is their Number One priority; their support has allowed Mayor Michael Bloomberg to increase education spending. But how will a middle-class Queens mother feel about paying ever-higher property taxes for more education spending when she knows that under the new funding rules, her child won't benefit proportionally from those taxes?

## FSF Is Not Fair for Some

Of course, middle-class parents might not mind spending their tax dollars on "fair student funding" if the program actually works. Most people want the poor to get ahead. But history shows that success for the new program is far from assured. Under the old system, while 28 percent of kids in the worst-funded elementary and middle schools were "low academic achievers," according to the Department of Education and the IBO, nearly 28 percent did just as poorly at the best-funded schools. At high schools, 36 percent of students did poorly at the worst-funded schools, versus 32 percent at the best-funded, the IBO's data show.

If the new system doesn't produce results, middle-class taxpayers might not be the only upset parents. Imagine that you're the single, working-poor parent of a middle-school student who scores low on standardized tests and is stuck in special education all day for years on end, with little improvement. It might dawn on you that your kid is a cash cow for the school—and you might demand that the politicians put your child's money to use somewhere else, maybe as a tuition payment at a parochial school. That would make "fair student funding" an even more radical reform than its advocates intend.

> *"Much of the reallocated money under the 65 percent requirement would go for better pay for teachers, which is wiser than just adding more teachers."*

# The 65 Percent Solution Is Essential to Improve Education

## George F. Will

*George F. Will is an author and syndicated political columnist. In the following viewpoint, he praises the increasingly popular 65 Percent Solution, which requires that 65 percent of every school district's education operational budget be spent on class-room instruction. Will argues that the 65 Percent Solution will more efficiently allocate resources and reward better teachers.*

As you read, consider the following questions:

1. What percentage of education operational budgets reach the classrooms now, according to Will?

2. Which four states does the author claim spend at least 65 percent of their budgets in classrooms?

3. According to the author, where would much of the real-located money under the 65 percent requirement go?

Patrick Byrne, a 42-year-old bear of a man who bristles with ideas that have made him rich and restless, has an idea that can provide a new desktop computer for every student in America without costing taxpayers a new nickel. Or it could provide 300,000 new $40,000-a-year teachers without any increase in taxes. His idea—call it the 65 Percent Solution—is politically delicious because it unites parents, taxpayers and teachers while, he hopes, sowing dissension in the ranks of the teachers unions, which he considers the principal institutional impediment to improving primary and secondary education.

## What Is the 65 Percent Solution?

The idea, which will face its first referendum in Arizona, is to require that 65 percent of every school district's education operational budget be spent on classroom instruction. On, that is, teachers and pupils, not bureaucracy.

Nationally, 61.5 percent of education operational budgets reach the classrooms. Why make a fuss about 3.5 percent? Because it amounts to $13 billion. Only four states (Utah, Tennessee, New York, Maine) spend at least 65 percent of their budgets in classrooms. Fifteen states spend less than 60 percent. The worst jurisdiction—Washington, D.C., of course—spends less than 50 percent.

Under the 65 percent rule, Arizona, which spends 56.8 percent in classrooms, could use its $451 million transfer to classrooms to buy 1.5 million computers or to hire 11,275 teachers. California (61.7 percent) could use its $1.5 billion transfer to buy 5 million computers or to hire 37,500 teachers. Illinois (59.5 percent) would transfer $906 million to classrooms (3 million computers or 22,650 new teachers). . . .

## Patrick Byrne's Mission

Byrne, who lives in Utah and has made a bundle in various business ventures, was once advised by Warren Buffett to pretend he is a batter at the plate with no one calling balls and strikes, so he can wait for a perfect pitch—a perfect idea. The 65 Percent Solution is perfect because it wins 80-plus percent support in polls and torments people who Byrne thinks should be tormented.

Buffett also advised him to ask himself this: If you had a silver bullet, what competitor would you shoot, and why? Byrne says he would shoot the National Education Association—the largest teachers union. Byrne is pugnacious—after graduating from Dartmouth, studying moral philosophy at Cambridge and earning a doctorate at Stanford, he tried a boxing career—and relishes the prospect of the 65 percent requirement pitting teachers against other union members who are in the education bureaucracy. "Educrats," he says, "have become what city hall was 50 or 60 years ago"—dens of patronage and corruption.

## Investing in Better Teachers

The 65 Percent Solution solves the misallocation of resources, but there is scant evidence that increasing financial inputs will by itself increase a school's cognitive outputs. Or that a small reduction in class size accomplishes much. Or that adding thousands of new teachers would do as much good as firing thousands of tenured incompetents.

However, firing a bad teacher is, according to a California official, less a choice than a career—figure two years of struggle and $200,000 in legal costs. That is why in a recent five-year period only 62 of California's 220,000 tenured teachers were dismissed.

Much of the reallocated money under the 65 percent requirement would go for better pay for teachers, which is wiser than just adding more teachers. Chester Finn, senior fellow at the Hoover Institution, notes that, while the number of pupils grew 50 percent in the past half-century, the number of teachers grew almost 300 percent. That pleased dues-collecting teachers unions and tuition-charging education schools. But if the number of teachers had grown apace with enrollments, and school budgets had risen as they have, teachers' salaries today would average nearly $100,000 instead of less than half that.

America, says Finn, has invested in more rather than better teachers—at a time when career opportunities were expanding for the able women who once were the backbone of public education. The fact that teachers' salaries have just kept pace with inflation, in spite of enormous expansions of school budgets, explains why too often teachers are drawn "from the lower ranks of our lesser universities."

Arizona's House speaker and Senate president have endorsed the 65 percent requirement, which should encounter scant opposition here or in the other 49 states to which Byrne's organization, First Class Education, is coming.

*"Put simply, the common-sense belief that directing more money to classrooms helps kids learn is not borne out by the data."*

# The 65 Percent Solution Is a Flawed Allocation System

**Susan Phillips**

*Susan Phillips is the former executive director of Connect for Kids, an education company. In the following viewpoint, she outlines both sides of the debate over the 65 Percent Solution, a proposed school funding formula. Phillips agrees with researchers and analysts who oppose the proposal because such a funding system can be easily manipulated, is a distraction to achieving better results, and hinders the ability of educational reformers to make important changes.*

As you read, consider the following questions:

1. Across the United States, what percentage of their budgets do school districts spend on "in the classroom" expenses, according to the author?

2. According to Phillips, how much money would the 65 Percent Solution shift to classrooms annually?

3. What is the position of the national PTA on the 65 Percent Solution, in the author's view?

A cross the U.S., school districts spent an average of 61.3 percent of their budgets on "in the classroom" expenses, as defined by the National Center for Education Statistics (NCES). In some districts, the figure is much lower, below 50 percent.

Recently, an organization called First Class Education (FCE) has been pushing a simple proposal: require school districts to increase "in the classroom" expenditures by 2 percent a year until they reach 65 percent. FCE argues that this is a simple, common-sense approach that requires school districts to focus their resources on children in classrooms rather than administration and overhead. The group estimates that nationwide adoption of the 65 percent standard would shift $14 billion a year—enough for a new computer for every student in the country or 300,000 new teachers (at $40,000 per year).

## How the 65 Percent Solution Polls

"It's overwhelmingly popular. It appeals to everybody," says Tim Mooney, a Republican consultant heading up FCE's Washington, DC office. He cited polling carried out by Harris Interactive for FCE and released in November 2005. "There is not a single demographic subset that is less than three-to-one in favor, no matter how you slice it: 78 percent of Republicans, 81 percent of Democrats, 89 percent of Hispanics, 96 percent of African Americans."

"My general reaction is this is sort of seductive but seriously oversimplified and possibly harmful," says Chester Finn, president of the Thomas B. Fordham Foundation and self-described education policy wonk [expert]. "It's seductive for all the obvious reasons: it meets the test of common sense that two-thirds of school dollars should be spent in class-rooms, and speaks to the feeling that it is both astonishing and alarming that this is not the case." But, warns Finn, "It's a blunt mechanism that is insensitive to underlying problems."

## The Fine Print

First Class Education says its goal is to have the 65 percent solution passed either as legislation or through ballot initiatives in all 50 states and the District of Columbia by the end of 2008. The campaign got a big boost from a George Will column published in April 2005.

The plan is straightforward: it uses the National Center for Education Statistics' definition for "in the classroom" expenses that would qualify for the 65 percent share:

- classroom teachers and aides;

- general instructional supplies;

- instructional aides;

- activities (field trips, athletics, music, arts);

- special needs instruction;

- tuition paid to out-of-state districts and private institutions for special needs students.

"Outside the classroom expenses" which would be competing for the remaining 35 percent are:

- administration (salaries and expenses);

- building operations and maintenance;

- food services;

- transportation;

- instructional staff support;

- student support (nurses, therapists, guidance counselors).

The NCES definition, which was created some 30 years ago, excludes school libraries and librarians, while covering such things as coaches and uniforms. (The American Library Association is urging states considering the measure to use the No Child Left Behind [a 2002 education law] definition of instructional staff which does include librarians and media specialists.) Similarly, speech/language pathologists and other specialists who work with learning disabled students are not included, though special education teachers are. Teacher training is excluded.

Districts that spend less than 65 percent of their budgets on "in the classroom" expenses would have to come up with plans to increase the percentage they spend by two percent a year until 65 percent is reached. If district officials feel they can't reach that goal, they could apply for a one-year waiver, which could be renewed.

## The Rationale

A driving force behind the 65 percent solution is entrepreneur Patrick Byrne, the founder of Overstock.com, who has pledged $1 million toward the effort. Byrne has told reporters that the idea came to him after looking at 2002–2003 data from NCES which showed that the five states with the highest student standardized test scores—Massachusetts, New Hampshire, Vermont, Minnesota and Connecticut—spent on average just over 64 percent in the classroom. The five worst-scoring states—Louisiana, Alabama, Mississippi, New Mexico and the District of Columbia—spent on average 59.5 percent.

Critics say Byrne's thinking ignores other factors—such as the fact that high performing states generally spend more overall per student, and that low performing states not only spend less, but have more poor and minority students.

But supporters say it comes down to common sense and good management. Brian Janssen is leading the effort to get the 65 percent solution on the ballot in Washington state for November 2006. Janssen, former Microsoft Corp. employee who later co-founded Onyx Software, is now a stay-at-home dad with three young children who is active in philanthropic causes.

"I feel strongly about public education," says Janssen. "My parents were public school teachers. . . . When we started our software company, we ran it very leanly. We had to do things efficiently, and we had to prioritize. It was an enormous challenge but a very healthy exercise to go through."

## Pushing Reform

Janssen says that he's discouraged by the quality of Seattle public schools. "I've seen over the last years so many extreme examples of waste and bad decision-making," says Janssen. As a donor to various charitable organizations, "I always tell the executive director of that organization, 'You really have a moral imperative to achieve the maximum effect with every dollar you receive from a donor.' I feel the same holds true for public education dollars."

In Washington state, says Janssen, 59.5 cents on every dollar go to "in the classroom" expenditures. "I am completely confident that our districts could do better, if they really looked at competitive bidding, sharing services." He questions whether the state really needs 296 districts, some of them very small. And he suggests adoption of a statewide curriculum would stop every district from "reinventing the wheel."

Though teachers' unions oppose the measure, Janssen insists that as he travels the state, individual teachers are enthusiastic and often give him examples of wasteful spending. "There's a never-ending call for more money for education from teachers' unions, sometimes quite justified," says Janssen. "But how much is enough?"

## But Will It Work?

The proposal is seen skeptically by many researchers and analysts who have spent years researching school finance and governance and student achievement.

Eric Hanushek, a senior fellow at the Hoover Institution, is an economist who has spent decades "trying to understand why some kids learn more than others, how you can increase achievement, how policies and finance interact with student performance and outcomes."

He terms the 65 percent solution "a great sound bite," and worries that it will become a distraction. "We are now finally at a stage where we are paying a lot more attention to whether kids are learning something," says Hanushek, referring to the new national emphasis on accountability. "It seems much more sensible to continue to concentrate on that, to hold districts responsible for improving achievement, and to help them do it."

"I understand wanting to cut down on the blob of bureaucracy," says Hanushek, but he argues that any measure that looks only at inputs—i.e., where the dollars go—without also tracking outputs—how students perform—is fundamentally flawed.

## Critics Worry About the Plan in Practice

Jane Hannaway, director of education policy at the Urban Institute, studies how school districts allocate their funds. She says that the 65 percent rule "is not a very refined school reform effort and can easily be gamed."

More importantly, it can reduce the ability of reformers to act. Hannaway has done research on San Diego's successful school reform efforts. She notes that the architects of that reform, Alan Bersin and Tony Alvarado, centralized a lot of discretionary funding—such as federal Title I funding—to pay for rigorous professional development of their principals and teachers. Then, "Once everyone was on the same page, they started sending money back to the schools," says Hannaway. The 65 percent solution would make it difficult to carry out such a plan.

## A Simple Solution to a Complex Problem

At first glance, a campaign by the First Class Education organization to require all states to spend 65 percent of every education dollar on in-classroom instruction sounds like something educators would be racing to embrace.

Tim Mooney, director of First Class Education and a political consultant in Arizona, said the campaign is all about making the classroom the first priority for educational spending.

But while First Class Education's proposal, also dubbed the 65 Percent Solution, is being supported by many state lawmakers, its harshest critics are national education organizations. Opponents have called it a political gimmick, and an unscientific one-size-fits-all formula whose narrow definition of instructional expenses will squeeze necessary support services out of schools.

"It's a simple solution to a complex problem," said Dr. Paul Houston, executive director of the American Association of School Administrators.

"Politicians love simple solutions. But they shouldn't be allowed to pass simple solutions until they understand complex problems."

*Ellen R. Delisio,*
*"65 Percent Solution: Gimmick or Gold Mine,"*
Education World, *April 13, 2007.*

In 2005, Standard & Poor's analyzed school spending in nine states that are considering implementing the 65 percent solution. The S&P report, issued last fall, found "no significant relationship between instructional spending at 65 percent or any other level and student performance."

Put simply, the common-sense belief that directing more money to classrooms helps kids learn is not borne out by the data.

Fordham's Finn believes the whole focus on kids in classrooms is outdated anyway. "I'm very pumped about online learning, virtual learning, all the ways that the education of kids is going to occur outside the four walls of the traditional classroom . . . to confine spending to those four walls might actually retard that kind of change."

## Politics, Politics

The momentum that the 65 percent solution has gained in certain states seems to be tightly linked to partisan politics on the ground.

Mooney has acknowledged being the author of a memo that outlines the advantages of the proposal for Republicans. In states with the issue on the ballot, the memo says, Republican candidates will be able to champion a popular measure to increase classroom spending without raising taxes. Another plus: The proposal "naturally puts administrators and teachers at odds with one another. . . . Because most state education unions represent both administrators and teachers, the proposal will create tremendous tension." In a recent interview, Mooney also said that the measure is more popular among Republican governors and candidates for state office than among Democrats.

The National PTA issued a position statement opposing the 65 percent solution in January. "This is consistent with a position we have that supports local control of how schools are funded. We feel that local school boards and districts know best," says National PTA President Anna Marie Weselak. "Sixty-five percent may work in some districts, but not in others."

While the National PTA claims about 6 million members, Weselak notes that it is up to local PTAs to decide if and how they will be active on the issue if it comes up in their state.

Mooney dismisses the National PTA as "a furtherance of the teachers' unions. . . . It just shows you how out of step with the American public, the American taxpayer and the American parent these organizations are."

> "The [Race to the Top] program awards grant money to states on a competitive basis, . . . turning around worst-performing schools, and recruiting and rewarding quality teachers."

# The Race to the Top Competition Spurs Educational Reform

*Kevin D. Teasley*

*Kevin D. Teasley is the president of the Greater Educational Opportunities Foundation. In the following viewpoint, he discusses the potential benefits of president Barack Obama's Race to the Top program, such as educational reforms that establish stricter accountability and competition within school systems. Teasley argues that the Race to the Top program has a long way to go but is on track to achieve great results.*

As you read, consider the following questions:

1. How much did president Barack Obama announce the federal government was planning to spend on his Race to the Top program, according to the author?

2. How did legislators in the author's home state of Indiana respond to the prospect of Race to the Top funds?

3. Why does the author believe that Race to the Top will succeed where other programs have failed?

A week ago [in January 2010], President Obama announced that he is planning to spend $4.4 billion on his Race to the Top education program. If you missed the news, don't kick yourself. Obama's entire education reform plan had been largely overshadowed by the yearlong health care debate, the economy, Afghanistan and other big-ticket news items.

It's unfortunate, since this may be the most impressive reform his administration has accomplished in the past year.

Obama announced Race to the Top in July [2009]. The program awards grant money to states on a competitive basis, based on their implementing education reforms that include assessment standards, turning around worst-performing schools, and recruiting and rewarding quality teachers.

Education Secretary Arne Duncan has met with education leaders throughout the country, working tirelessly to get state education leaders and providers, legislators, reform groups, unions and others to support reforms that will bring true accountability and competition to our nation's public school systems.

The result has been remarkable.

## The Competition Begins

States across the country worked feverishly during the 2009 legislative session, pushing through reforms that set up stricter accountability, implement merit pay programs for teachers and allow more competition within the school system. Reforms, it's worth noting, that the teaching establishment has long resisted.

In my home state of Indiana, for example, legislators responded to the prospect of $250 million in grants by halting their desire to place caps on charter schools while changing

## Race to the Top Winners

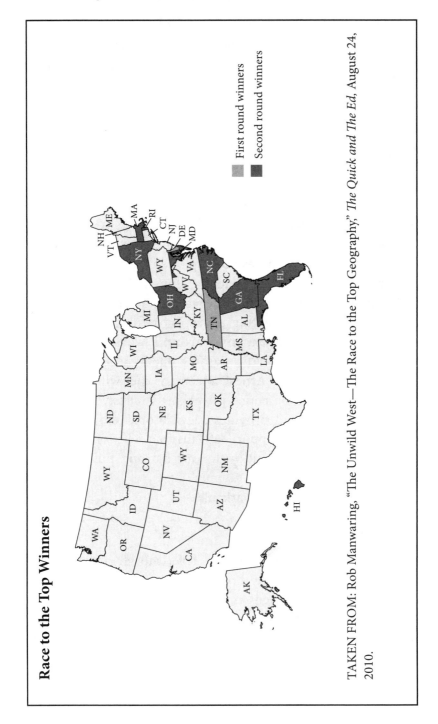

TAKEN FROM: Rob Manwaring, "The Unwild West—The Race to the Top Geography," *The Quick and The Ed,* August 24, 2010.

the licensing process and requirements. The state is also looking at merit pay programs as well as grading schools according to their performance. (It was interesting to see the state's Republican governor and Republican state education superintendent quote the Obama/Duncan plans to state Democrats.) Indiana school districts, meanwhile, are reviewing the process of contracting with charter management organizations to manage their lowest-performing schools.

Other states looking to gain access to these competitive grants are implementing similar reforms. For example, the *New York Times* reported earlier this month that California and Wisconsin repealed laws that had banned linking student achievement data to teachers. And California passed a law that lets parents move children out of low-performing districts.

## Why Race to the Top Is Different

Of course, the desire for accountability and competition is not new, and in fact has been tried by numerous Republican administrations. But to a great extent, they failed.

But today the promise of accountability and competition is likely to be realized, primarily because Obama and Duncan are the right messengers. With Obama/Duncan leading the charge, the usual suspects who stand in the schoolhouse door blocking reform are having a tough time standing up, let alone finding the door.

How will this all end up? The reality is that no one actually knows. The country has a long, long way to go before it can claim to have made meaningful progress on education reform. And the success of this program depends heavily on how it's implemented.

But I think it's safe to say that the Race to the Top program is on track to achieve great returns for the taxpayers' investment. The policy changes that have already taken place in state after state are encouraging.

Now, let's see the results in improved academic achievement.

> "The administration opted for a competition that primarily rewarded grant-writing prowess . . . rather than concrete structural changes."

# The Race to the Top Competition Does Not Result in Necessary Reforms

## Frederick M. Hess

*Frederick M. Hess is an author and the director of education policy studies at the American Enterprise Institute. In the following viewpoint, he maintains that the Race to the Top winners do not reflect the true state of education reform in states throughout the country. Hess asserts that mediocre states won the competition, while states implementing compelling and successful reforms did not.*

As you read, consider the following questions:

1. What states were among the winners of the second round of Race to the Top, according to the author?

2. What states were the winners of the first round of Race to the Top, according to the author?

3. How much funding for Race to the Top did the Barack Obama administration request for 2011, according to Hess?

That was another $4.35 billion poorly spent. Last week [August 2010], Secretary of Education Arne Duncan announced the winners of the second and final round of the [Barack Obama] administration's heavily promoted and widely cheered Race to the Top school-reform program. Unfortunately, after all the headlines and hullabaloo, the results were so dismal they threatened to bring the entire exercise into disrepute. Heralded education-reform states Colorado and Louisiana were left out in the cold, while Duncan bizarrely found himself naming Ohio, Maryland, New York, and Hawaii among the ten round-two winners. (Tennessee and Delaware had been named round-one winners this spring.)

## Reforms Do Not Lead to Victory

Several of the winners clearly trail the pack on key reforms that Duncan had said RTT would reward. When it comes to state data systems, the Data Quality Campaign has ranked the states: Hawaii tied for 17th, Maryland tied for 35th, and New York tied for 48th. When it comes to the clarity and strength of the states' charter laws, the National Alliance for Public Charter Schools has rated Ohio 26th, Hawaii 34th, and Maryland 40th. On teacher policy, the National Council on Teacher Quality has graded the states, with Ohio and New York each earning a D+, Maryland a D, and Hawaii a D−.

Meanwhile, less than a month ago, Duncan described Louisiana as "leading the way" with data systems that monitor teacher-preparation programs and student performance. Louisiana has been ranked a top-ten state for teacher policy, data systems, and charter schooling. Colorado enacted the single most important piece of legislation to come out of the RTT process—its remarkable Senate Bill 191, which overhauled teacher evaluation and tenure and introduced a smart state-wide framework for gauging teacher performance. (In announcing the results, Duncan did say that Colorado "will continue to be a national leader." Presumably, it will just have to lead from the rear.)

## Race to the Top Does Not Reflect True Reform

Conservative education analyst Chester E. Finn Jr. concluded that the review process didn't reflect "what's really going on in these states and the degree of sincerity of their reform convictions." Andy Rotherham, veteran [Bill] Clinton education hand and key Democratic education thinker, acknowledged that there were "raised eyebrows"; specifically, he anticipated questions about "how New York went from not meeting the absolute priority for the competition to being a winner," and noted concerns about "reviewers that didn't reflect the administration's avowed reform priorities." Colorado's lieutenant governor, Barbara O'Brien, fumed, "You can't say it's an objective process. . . . I just have no confidence in this process the U.S. Department of Education has put together."

This was largely a bed of Duncan's own making. Last year, the administration opted for a competition that primarily rewarded grant-writing prowess and allegiance to the fads of the moment rather than concrete structural changes. Skeptics warned that the administration's hurriedly assembled contest was not equal to the weight it was being asked to bear and raised questions about the murky criteria for judge selection, ambiguity of the scoring process, emphasis on promises rather than accomplishments, and preference for "inclusive" efforts rather than focused ones.

## The Role of Teachers' Unions

Moreover, when announcing round-one winners Tennessee and Delaware in March, Duncan took pains to note that the

## Criticism of Race to the Top

Announced in July, the nationwide competition [Race to the Top] offers states a chance to get a windfall of funds if they meet certain eligibility criteria. Among the 19 requirements are developing and implementing common statewide standards and data systems and increasing the availability of charter schools. . . .

Initial guidelines for the money drew about 1,100 responses, with many offering support, yet some of the most heated comments came from teachers' unions.

In a 26-page letter, the NEA said they found the "top-down approach disturbing" and that the emphasis on data amounted to "ignoring states' rights to enact their own laws and constitutions."

*Nia-Malika Henderson,*
*"Teachers' Unions Uneasy with President Barack Obama,"*
Politico, *October 17, 2009.*

two states had had 100 percent or near 100 percent signoffs from their local teachers' unions. Not surprisingly, the judges followed Duncan's lead. Among the winners, North Carolina, Ohio, and Hawaii had 100 percent of their union locals signing off on their proposals, and New York had 70 percent doing so. States like Colorado and New Jersey got hammered for not collecting enough unenforceable assurances from their unions. An official from one losing state steamed, "To have peer reviewers praise the application up and down but still explicitly penalize us because of our union opposition is almost too much to bear."

The disheartening close of its prized program is bad news for the administration and probably signals rough seas ahead for its education agenda in 2011. Despite Duncan's expressed hope that "This may be the end of phase two, but it's not the end of Race to the Top," and the president's request for another $1.35 billion for RTT next year, it will be a surprise if Duncan gets to give this another try. Given that the president's standing on education has already fallen precipitously, with Gallup reporting this month that just 34 percent of adults give him an A or a B when grading his performance on education, the messy endgame may weaken the administration's credibility on reform. One respected charter-school advocate lamented, "With the inclusion of Maryland, North Carolina, and Ohio and the exclusion of Colorado and Louisiana, the administration has lost its ability to push states to make tough changes in matters like charter schools or teacher policies."

## Looking Ahead

In the meantime, Duncan now confronts a whole new headache. While the winning plans are mostly about grand promises, the cast of characters in most of those states is about to change. Half of the RTT winners will be inaugurating new governors come January, and four others may be doing so. In other words, ten of Duncan's twelve RTT winners may have new leaders in 2011. How wedded will these new governors be to the airy promises contained in the winning RTT applications? If and when they balk, the Obama administration will have two bad options.

Either Duncan will have to admit he handed out 4 billion borrowed bucks on the basis of unenforceable paper plans, or he'll have to start trying to strong-arm states by holding new governors and state education chiefs to the commitments of their predecessors—and clawing back dollars from states that don't comply. Neither of those scenarios is too appealing, especially in a year when a number of amped-up Republican gubernatorial candidates seem all too eager to tangle with the Obama administration.

> *"The research reveals that, all else equal, countries with national standards do no better than those without."*

# School Funding Should Not Be Tied to Establishing National Standards

*Neal McCluskey*

*Neal McCluskey is the associate director of the Cato Institute's Center for Educational Freedom. In the following viewpoint, he observes that the federal government is trying to link national curriculum standards to federal funds in the form of the Race to the Top program. McCluskey finds that many of the government's efforts have flown under the radar, and he asserts that if the US public heard about them, they would reject them.*

As you read, consider the following questions:

1. How many states does McCluskey say have capitulated to national math and language arts standards?

2. According to the author, why did the last push for national standards fail?

3. Why does the author believe that national curriculum standards are the biggest federal takeover you have never heard of?

There's a revolution happening, and you probably don't even know it. While you've been worrying about wars, spills, and bailouts, Washington has been taking over schools nationwide. So far, Virginia has resisted, but already more than 30 states have capitulated to national mathematics and language arts standards. And amazingly, almost no one's heard about this. But that's exactly what standardizers, who know national standards' fatal flaws, want.

## A National Bribery Scheme

The immediate impetus for this has been the Race to the Top (RTTT), a competition for $4.35 billion in federal funds. Adopting standards created by something called the Common Core State Standards Initiative [CCSSI] is crucial for states to compete.

In an impressive defense of state sovereignty, Virginia stayed out of the most recent round of RTTT, taking itself out of the federal bribery scheme. But many national-standards aficionados have been rhetorically abusing the commonwealth ever since, trying to get it blindly to follow the crowd.

Despite this, national standards have probably been flying almost as far under the radar in the commonwealth as elsewhere. Which raises the question: Why the secrecy?

The answer is that keeping this all hush-hush has been the key to national-standards proponents getting their way.

## CCSSI Strategy

The last national standards push—which included history, English, science, and other subjects—was in the 1990s, and it disintegrated almost the moment the first proposed standards

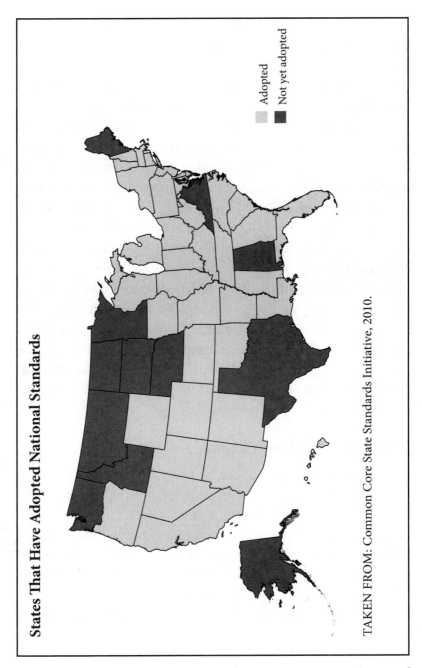

**States That Have Adopted National Standards**

Adopted

Not yet adopted

TAKEN FROM: Common Core State Standards Initiative, 2010.

were released. Everyone, it seemed, was paying attention, and every diverse American found something in the very detailed standards to hate.

Avoiding a similar public outcry explains why today the CCSSI has furnished only mathematics and language arts standards, and why the latter identify almost no specific works students must read. Math is relatively uncontroversial, as is English—if you don't prescribe any actual readings.

The problems, of course, are that focusing on just two subjects threatens to narrow the curriculum, while dodging essential reading would hollow it out. Do more, though, and Americans might have something of substance to grab onto.

Another reason for keeping things muted has been, it seems, to deceive the public about what—and who—is driving the standards. Contrary to proponents' incessant refrain, standardization has been neither "state led" nor "voluntary," and it's been the heavy hand of Washington [D.C.; i.e., the federal government] that's been shoving everything along.

While creation of the Common Core was spearheaded by associations of governors and state education chiefs, those groups do not represent individual states. Meanwhile, the National Conference of State Legislatures opposes national standards.

## The Next Step Toward Standardization

Of course, many state school boards have adopted the standards, but they might just be happily passing the standards buck. Much more important, thanks to RTTT and [Barack] Obama administration plans to connect national standards to even bigger piles of money—the latter will be the next honeypot offered to Virginia—adoption is no more "voluntary" than adhering to the No Child Left Behind Act [2002 education reform law] or the minimum drinking age. If states want federal dollars—which were taken from their citizens to begin with—they must do as they're told.

Finally, national standardizers have almost certainly tried to keep their efforts muffled because there is simply no meaningful evidence that national standards work. Despite proponents' superficial claims about needing national standards to compete in the world economy, or all countries that outperform us having such standards, the research reveals that, all else equal, countries with national standards do no better than those without. Research also reveals that the freer the education system—the more autonomous schools and consumers are—the better.

It's not hard to understand why. Government schooling is almost always controlled by the people it employs because they are the most motivated to be involved in education politics. And like most people, they would prefer as little outside accountability as possible. Conversely, more freedom means more competition, and that means real accountability—answering to customers—as well as constant innovation.

So why are national curriculum standards the biggest federal takeover you've never heard of? Because they need silence to win. And here's another big secret: Should Virginia ever succumb to national standards, national tests are likely coming next.

> *"Employing nationwide standards, and the tests that go with them, is practically the only way we've come up with to ensure accountability."*

# Tying Federal Funds to National Standards Will Improve Education

*Erik Bryan*

*Erik Bryan is a writer and editor of textbooks and an associate editor of the online magazine the* Morning News. *In the following viewpoint, he maintains that the creation of a national set of standards may not fix all of the problems in education, but it could at least create a more even playing field for small states. By addressing the inequalities found in existing state standards, national standards would provide a clear and consistent criteria for educators and textbook publishers.*

As you read, consider the following questions:

1. According to the author, why do textbook companies write books suited to the standards of larger states like Texas and New York?

2. What is the Common Core State Standards Initiative, according to Bryan?

3. Why does the author maintain that the Texas argument about states' rights is deceptive?

Most days I love my job. For two and a half years, I've worked in education publishing, first as a textbook proofreader, now as an editor and writer. Creating the materials students will use across the country to develop their skills in English is pretty awesome. I come from a family full of teachers, and probably would have become one myself were it not for a lifelong fear of teenagers. On the days I don't really love my job, though, there's one culprit: lousy state educational standards.

If you don't have children in public school, or if you haven't been in public school yourself in more than a decade, you may not know about "standards" in the official educational sense. Essentially, they're a set of guidelines drafted by bureaucrats, think tanks, and teachers, supposedly to help streamline the process for students to prepare for standardized tests. All states have their own standards, which they've drafted under different circumstances, by different bureaucrats, think tanks, and teachers.

## The Business of Educational Publishing

As an editor and writer of textbooks, I'm affected because many of the larger states (e.g., California, Texas, Florida, New York) only purchase materials if their state standards are explicitly addressed and incorporated. As a result, education publishing companies are beholden to the big boys, and compete for their business by writing textbooks specifically suited to their needs.

Now, generally, the big states' standards are similar and, more importantly, sensible. In English language arts, they ask students to identify the characteristics of poetry, for instance, or to identify cause-and-effect relationships in works of fiction, or to demonstrate basic capabilities in reading comprehension. Easy enough. But sometimes, due to some states' poor standards quality, my job is very difficult. Like, extremely, frustratingly difficult. Like, throw-my-hands-up and get-up-for-a-walk-it-off-trip-to-the-water-cooler difficult. Sometimes a group of us editors—fairly well-educated adults, mind you—will convene around each others' desks just trying to make sense of what we're reading.

For standards to be useful to educators and people like me they must be clear, concise, and not only teachable, but testable. Many standards that I am currently forced to incorporate in my work are none of the above.

Remember when President George W. Bush asked, "Is our children learning?" That was a bad question. Mainly because I wish he'd said, "*What* is our children learning?"

## The Rise of Accountability

Almost all available data show standards-based education raises student performance. If you teach students according to standards, they perform better on standardized tests. Some argue that's a rather self-fulfilling prophecy, but it works on paper. The magic word behind the *need* for standards (as opposed to the *want* to use them to raise student scores) is "accountability."

My brother, Trevor, a Master's student in education, ominously puts it this way: The Rise of Accountability has taken over American education. Accountability means that if we're spending tax dollars, we need to be sure what we're doing is working, and to create an educational environment that can be measured by statistical analysis.

As Trevor says, "Accountability sucks, because it pushes everyone to the center of the curve. But you gotta have it." Employing nationwide standards, and the tests that go with them, is practically the only way we've come up with to ensure accountability.

## No Child Left Behind

Most states had picked up on the standards trend during the past few decades, reworking their public schools. Then, in 2002, President Bush signed the bipartisan-supported No Child Left Behind (or N.C.L.B.) Act into law. The act stipulated that a lot of federal money (about $17 billion at the time; increased in 2007 to more than $24 billion) would be distributed to state schools provided that those schools (a) implemented standards-based education and (b) raised reading and math performance on standardized tests incrementally, year by year (which, in the language of the act, is known as proving "adequate yearly progress," or AYP). States could pick their own standards, which made them happy as they sniffed their new moneybags. However, schools that failed to meet AYP would be put on a watch list. And if they couldn't get off that list in less than five years, the school would face restructuring, which could mean faculty firings or student transfers. All in the name of accountability.

Nearly 10 years later, the most serious complaints about N.C.L.B. converge around two issues. The first is that, in order to meet adequate yearly progress, many state school systems gradually lowered their standards. This made it easier for schools to get passing grades, but it did nothing to ensure that students could compete at a national level, or later at college, or in their careers. This is the "race to the bottom" that so many educators and legislators have identified.

The second problem with N.C.L.B. is that, even with some schools trying to "juke the stats," in the parlance of *The Wire* [a TV drama], about a third of America's public schools still failed to meet AYP in the 2008–09 school year. That number is rising. The law is simply not producing its desired results.

## Creating National Standards

Without further details, it remains to be seen whether president [Barack] Obama's blueprint to reform education will fix the increase in so-called failing schools. However, a couple of weeks ago, I read of a current effort to create a national set of testing standards for English and math curricula. The Common Core State Standards Initiative—led by a panel compiled from the National Governors Association and the Council of Chief State School Officers—intends to correct the inequalities found in existing state standards, which, as a skeptical textbook editor with muted rage issues, I think is fantastic.

Some state standards are crap. Here are examples: From Texas, we find the following standards in Grade 4 of the Texas Essential Knowledge Skills. One is that students must "seek clarification of spoken language as needed." This is difficult to teach because you're relying on students to ask for clarification—but just because they don't ask doesn't mean they don't need it. And whether or not it's teachable, it's certainly not testable; students are never allowed to ask for clarification in a standardized testing environment.

Another Texas standard says students must "understand the general meaning of spoken language ranging from situations in which contexts are familiar to unfamiliar." This standard is vague in its wording, and includes a false range (in this case, "familiar to unfamiliar") that is exceedingly difficult to determine at any given point in time—as in, say, a test setting. Finally, we find that students should "use accessible language and learn new and essential language in the process." Nowhere do they bother to define what they think accessible language is, and I'm left to assume essential language is something like, "Can I use the bathroom now?"

Whatever the meaning of the terms to define these standards, it's hard to prove by testing that students are meeting them. Texas isn't the only state guilty of gobbledygook. South

Carolina third graders are expected to "read independently for extended periods of time for pleasure." How do they teach this? How do you test it?

## The Case of New York State

The Grade 8 New York English Language Arts Core Curriculum standards for listening comprehension skills insist that students must "respect the age, gender, social position, and cultural traditions of the speaker," "withhold judgment," and "appreciate the speaker's uniqueness." I've spent whole afternoons slamming my head on my desk writing practice tests, trying to come up with questions to address these requirements. I see wording like this in my nightmares. While these standards signal valuable, if not lofty, intentions for teenagers, they are almost impossible to assess in a standardized testing environment. Being asked to develop preparatory tests that align with these well-meaning, untestable standards is the hardest part of my job. Actually testing students on these dubious standards does them no great service, either.

My friend Sarah, a New York City public high school teacher, told me, "New York state standards are pretty much meaningless." She feels standards should play a part in public education, and they need revising—but the bigger problem is when AYP-failing schools (often in poor, urban areas) are punished for not meeting existing benchmarks. Teachers occasionally encourage poor-performing students to leave public school altogether, Sarah says, so as not to negatively influence the school's score.

She also cites a taxing mix of unhelpful parents, rigid teachers who refuse to comply with new legislation, and the fact that schools in poor districts are being forced to accommodate unique social issues—like children who can't afford lunch, or don't have homes to return to after school—as evidence that whatever happens with standards, revising them is not going to do the job alone of improving our national educational standards—not the official "standards," but the standard we should expect of a great country.

But one thing at a time.

## The Problem with National Standards

Some states have expressed trepidation over the adoption of national standards. Their fears are not without merit. As Jim Stergios of a Boston non-profit involved in revising Massachusetts state standards said, "Ours in Massachusetts are much higher, so why should we adopt [national standards]?" Texas and Alaska have opted out of the national standard adoption process altogether, with Texas Gov. Rick Perry arguing that Texans should decide what Texans learn.

The stand that this is a states' rights issue is, in the case of Texas in particular, disingenuous. As one of the largest states, with one of the biggest public school systems, the standards set for Texas schools have a way of drawing attention (and human capital) from major publishers in a way few other states can. In fact, many publishers remain in business by aligning their core educational curricula to Texas standards and selling virtually identical textbooks nationally—an issue that caught attention recently due to the intense debate over Texas's social studies and history standards.

If national standards pass for English and math, other subjects could follow, including science, social studies, and history. The big states that have previously managed to direct the course of education publishing with their market share may no longer retain that power. The effect would be that smaller states wouldn't have to put up with any particular state's flights of fancy, political or otherwise, and editors like me won't spend hours trying to shoehorn smaller states' round-peg standards into bigger states' square holes.

## The Current System Must Be Revised

My stepfather, Blair, became a teacher in 1974 and has taught everything from kindergarten to university-level humanities and music theory courses. He uses the analogy of comparing apples and oranges when different state's standards are juxtaposed. He is very concerned about the move in our country toward "high-stakes testing," as he puts it, because he fears what education can provide and accomplish for students is narrowing.

He also worries about efforts currently under way in many states to force a standardized testing mold onto other subjects, like music or art, that simply won't fit, devaluing music and art teachers professionally. However, Blair points out that since proficiency in many subjects *can* be tested, these subjects should share standards at a national level so that all students are considered equally. This would ensure some assumptions could be made about what each student knows when entering a new grade, or a new school district. As he eloquently puts it, "Knowledge is not a local issue." . . .

An accountability- and standards-based form of education isn't going away—but the current system is unworkable and needs revising. Having a national set of standards may not fix many of our system's problems, but it could provide a relatively simple tweak that sets the playing field a little more evenly for students in public schools.

It will also, I hope, make my job a little easier.

# Periodical and Internet Sources Bibliography

*The following articles have been selected to supplement the diverse views presented in this chapter.*

| | |
|---|---|
| Arlene Ackerman | "Mike's School Funding Fix Worked out West," *New York Daily News*, March 29, 2007. |
| Dave Arnold | "Our Enemies Never Rest," National Education Association, 2008. |
| Lindsey Burke | "Empower Parents, Not 'Educrats,' to Improve Schools," The Heritage Foundation, August 25, 2010. |
| *Grand Rapids Press* | "Don't Stop Race to the Top Education Reform," August 3, 2010. |
| Dan Lips | "A Smarter Path to a 'Race to the Top' in Education Reform," The Heritage Foundation, January 26, 2010. |
| Patricia A. Lynch | "Race to the Top Program Just Too Murky for Teachers to Accept," *Dayton Daily News*, January 20, 2010. |
| *New York Times* | "National School Standards at Last," March 13, 2010. |
| *New York Times* | "Continue the Race," August 28, 2010. |
| *Orange County Register* | "Dumbing Down for Race to the Top," August 9, 2010. |
| Robert Panning-Miller | "What's Wrong with Race to the Top, and What's Right with Minnesota Schools," *Twin Cities Daily Planet*, April 10, 2010. |
| Marcus Winters | "Race to the Top Program Prioritizes Reform," *Washington Examiner*, December 16, 2009. |

# CHAPTER 3

# How Successful Have Recent Funding Initiatives Been?

# Chapter Preface

One of the hottest trends in American education during the past few decades is the establishment of charter schools. In areas with charter schools, a student's family can choose the school that best fits that child's particular needs, such as those with an emphasis on art, math and science, Head Start, or troubled children. Charter schools receive public money but are allowed to operate without many of the regulations that apply to traditional public schools. Charter schools are one of the fastest-growing innovations in education policy, garnering bipartisan support from governors, state legislators, and past and present secretaries of education. Charter schools have more autonomy with issues such as class size, teaching practices, and curricula as long as they still deliver positive academic results and maintain fiscal responsibility. Although the popularity of charter schools has increased dramatically over the past twenty years and the US Department of Education considers them a key part of any educational reform attempts, critics argue that charter schools are not the panacea that many education officials consider them to be. That has not stopped the charter school movement from growing: in 2009 more than 1.5 million students were enrolled in more than five thousand charter schools in forty-one states and Puerto Rico.

The charter school movement grew from a number of reform ideas that originated in the 1960s and 1970s. Educators all over the country were experimenting with alternative schools, public school choice, privatization, and community-parental empowerment. In the 1970s, a New England educator, Ray Budde, came up with the idea of school boards giving contracts, or charters, to small groups of reform-minded teachers to try innovative teaching practices in their classrooms. Other reformers seized upon the idea and suggested that local school boards could charter an entire school as long as teachers and unions were willing collaborators. One of the most influential voices supporting the movement was Albert Shanker, president of the American Federation of Teachers, who called for the reform of public schools through the creation of "schools of choice" or "charter schools" in 1988. With the growing support of unions, educators, and politicians, the charter school movement began to spread. In the late 1980s several charter schools were created in Philadelphia—and many of those were schools of choice. It was Minnesota, however, that really took the charter school movement to a new level. The state passed the first charter school law in 1991. A year later, California passed its own version. By 1995 nineteen states had passed laws that allowed charter schools. In 2009 there were forty-one.

Commentators trace the popularity of charter schools to their three core values: choice, accountability, and freedom. Charter schools must perform to the goals set in their original charter, and they are judged by how well they meet those goals each school year. Finally, there is a level of freedom— innovation, experimentation, and flexibility—that exists in charter schools that is not found in more traditional public schools.

As the charter movement grows, however, so does the controversy surrounding it. As critics point out, less supervision and regulation can lead to problems. In the worst cases, there have been underperforming schools and troubling fiscal mismanagement. According to 2009 data from the Center for Education Reform, 657 of the more than 5,250 charter schools opened have been closed for a variety of reasons.

Critics also point to a wide body of evidence that shows that charter schools are no better than public schools academically. According to the National Assessment of Educational Progress, charter schools have never outperformed public schools. Studies have also shown that charter schools increase racial segregation.

The controversy over charter schools is just one of the topics explored in the following chapter, which looks at the performance of recent school funding initiatives. Also examined in the chapter are school vouchers, Head Start, No Child Left Behind, magnet schools, and the D.C. Opportunity Scholarship program.

> *"Florida's tax-credit scholarship program has helped all of the state's students, even those who opt not to use a voucher."*

# School Vouchers Save Money and Improve Education

## *Marcus A. Winters*

*Marcus A. Winters is a senior fellow at the Manhattan Institute for Policy Research. In the following viewpoint, he examines the successes of Florida's school voucher program. Winters argues that Florida's experience with vouchers demonstrates that such programs save money and improve the quality of education for both private and public school students.*

As you read, consider the following questions:

1. When did Florida's Corporate Tax-Credit Scholarship Program start, according to Winters?

2. How many Florida students does the author say took part in the Corporate Tax-Credit Scholarship Program?

3. According to the author, what is each voucher offered under Florida's tax-credit program worth?

Barring a sudden economic U-turn, last year's stimulus and this year's additional $10 billion education bail-out will only delay painful state budget cuts. A huge portion of most state budgets go to public schools, making them an obvious place for cash-strapped legislatures to turn for savings.

Schools across the nation are already cutting services and teachers despite the influx of stimulus dollars, and in most cases kids are worse off for it. But Florida's experience over the last decade has shown that there is one budget area that schools can cut to both save money and improve educational services: students. These tight fiscal times provide just one more reason for state legislatures to embrace school choice.

## Florida's Experience with School Choice

Started under the governorship of Jeb Bush, Florida's Corporate Tax-Credit Scholarship Program has paid for students to attend secular and parochial private schools since 2001. As its name suggests, the program is funded by corporate donations for which companies receive a dollar-for-dollar tax credit.

To be eligible for a voucher a student must come from a family with an income low enough to qualify for free- or reduced-price lunch. Last year [2009], nearly 29,000 students across the state used a voucher from this program to attend a private school. That number is sure to increase now that the state legislature has significantly lifted the cap on the program's enrollment.

Most state legislatures aren't in the mood to consider programs that siphon off corporate tax revenues. But corporate tax-credit voucher programs reduce state public school expenditures by far more than they cut tax receipts.

Each voucher offered under Florida's tax-credit program is worth $3,950. In comparison, taxpayers pay a total of $11,077 to educate the average student in a Florida public school. The voucher is worth only 77 percent of what public schools spend on instructional services alone.

## The Benefits of Vouchers

Full school choice programs, also known as tuition vouchers, provide parents with a portion of the public educational funding allotted for their child to attend school, and allows them to use those funds to attend the school of their choice. It gives them the fiscal authority to send their child to the educational institution that best suits their child, whether it is a religious or parochial school, another private school, or a neighborhood or magnet public school. These programs empower the family and, in so doing, infuse consumer accountability into the traditional public schools system. A few states offer choice scholarship programs specifically for students with special needs.

*"Ed Reform FAQs,"*
*Center for Education Reform,*
*www.edreform.com.*

## Economic Benefits of Florida's Experiment

The cost savings from vouchers are quite real. According to Florida's Office of Program Analysis and Government Accountability—the state equivalent to the federal Office of Management and Budget—each dollar foregone in corporate tax revenues due to the program saves the state about $1.49 in public school expenditures. Overall, the program saved Florida's taxpayers an estimated $36.2 million during the 2008–09 school year.

Now that the cap has been raised, those savings will surely grow. Only about 2 percent of eligible students in the state used a voucher last year.

## Providing Choice

Unlike other cost-saving measures, voucher programs don't eliminate services or force citizens into unwanted new arrangements. Vouchers address the truly perverse arrangement whereby states force taxpayers to cough up multimillion dollar premiums in order to keep kids from low-income families enrolled in public schools that they'd rather not attend.

Whether or not food stamps make good policy, no current user of that program would choose to exit it. But there are many thousands (perhaps millions) of parents who yearn to send their child to a private school but can't afford the tuition.

Parents are under no obligation to take the voucher. They can continue to send their kids to the local public school if they wish.

For parents, it's not important how much a school spends but how well it teaches their children. Many families opt to take the vouchers because they are fed up with ineffective, expensive public schools.

## Results from Florida

According to a recent evaluation of one program by Northwestern University economist David Figlio—who, it should be noted, is one of the few researchers whose reputation is unchallenged by either side of the education policy debate—students participating in Florida's tax-credit scholarship program are more likely to come from the state's lowest performing public schools and tend to be among the lowest performers within their school.

Vouchers are one of the precious few policies that not only save money but also improve learning outcomes. According to Figlio's study, students who use one of Florida's tax-credit vouchers do slightly better in math than their peers in public school.

## Vouchers Lead to Reform

In addition, consistent with other research, Figlio found that competition from the voucher program actually produced improvements in public schools. That is, Florida's tax-credit scholarship program has helped all of the state's students, even those who opt not to use a voucher to attend a private school.

There is no avoiding the fact that most state budget cuts will leave citizens worse off than before. In public education, however, there are still major efficiencies to be found. Voucher programs both help kids and save money. In these tight fiscal times, vouchers don't just make good policy, they make good sense.

> "One simple reason why voucher sup-
> porters have become disillusioned is
> that the programs haven't delivered on
> their promises."

# School Vouchers Fail to Improve Education

*Greg Anrig*

*Greg Anrig is the vice president for programs at the Century Foundation. In the following viewpoint, he asserts that conservatives are abandoning their support for school voucher programs because they have failed to achieve the results they had promised. Anrig also notes that the results show that the income of a student's family and the social and economic background of his or her classmates are by far the most important influences on his or her academic future—a problem that existing voucher programs do not address.*

As you read, consider the following questions:

1. According to Anrig, who first suggested the idea of school vouchers?

2. How has the author described the effect of school voucher programs on public schools?

Greg Anrig, "An Idea Whose Time Is Gone," *Washington Monthly*, April 2008. Reproduced by permission.

3. How did the Florida supreme court rule on its statewide voucher program in 2006, according to the author?

In 1955, the libertarian economist Milton Friedman proposed what was, for its time, a radical idea: that schoolchildren be given government-funded vouchers to enable them to attend private schools. As ubiquitous as the notion of "school choice" has since become, Friedman's suggestion didn't immediately catch on, remaining mostly confined to academia for well over a decade. Then, in the 1970s, Lyndon Johnson–era liberals connected with President [Richard] Nixon's Office of Economic Opportunity suggested that generous vouchers be provided to low-income students, hoping to increase funds available for poor students and promote racial integration. But a coalition of teachers unions and school administrators strenuously objected, and the idea went nowhere.

## School Voucher Movement

It wasn't until Ronald Reagan's election to the presidency in 1980 that the modern school voucher movement took shape. Reagan's own relatively modest voucher proposals were repeatedly rebuffed by Congress. However, his ascent unleashed a torrent of money into conservative think tanks and advocacy groups promoting policies that would advance the movement's agenda of weakening the government, and, by extension, the Democratic Party. Conservative activists like William J. Bennett, Jack Kemp, and Clint Bolick seized on vouchers as a particularly potent example, in part because they struck at the heart of the nation's most deeply established governmental activity—public schooling. If conservatives could show that private schools worked better than public ones, and that the introduction of competition improved entire school systems, that would advance their arguments for welfare rollbacks, Social Security privatization, and other initiatives to replace government programs with the free market.

Based on such thinking, the John M. Olin and the Lynde and Harry Bradley Foundations led the way in pouring millions of dollars into institutions and activities that promoted vouchers and school choice. By 1987, the notion of vouchers had become sufficiently commonplace that Bennett, who had become Reagan's secretary of education, observed: "When I started talking about choice a couple of years ago, it was still regarded as somewhat heretical. Now it seems to be the conventional wisdom." In 1990, the Wisconsin legislature launched the nation's first publicly financed voucher initiative to include private schools in Milwaukee, backed by Tommy Thompson, the reform-minded Republican governor; Annette "Polly" Williams, a liberal African American state legislator; and the pugnacious Michael S. Joyce, the head of the Milwaukee-based Bradley Foundation. The voucher idea received a further infusion of legitimacy that same year from a hugely influential book called *Politics, Markets, & America's Schools*, by the scholars John E. Chubb and Terry M. Moe. Although the book was funded by the Olin and Bradley Foundations, it was published by the liberal Brookings Institution, where Chubb was a senior fellow. This affiliation suggested, misleadingly, that their argument wasn't rooted in right-wing ideology.

## Voucher Popularity Rises and Falls

Throughout the 1990s and the early part of this decade, voucher advocates sustained the offensive, gaining increasing support from African Americans such as Colin Powell and the prominent civil rights activist and mayor of Atlanta, Andrew Young; and Democrats such as Robert Reich, who believed that a radical experiment like vouchers was worth trying after the failure of more traditional reforms to produce functional urban school systems. After a favorable state supreme court ruling in 1998, Milwaukee's voucher experiment was expanded, from about fifteen hundred students attending less than two dozen secular schools to more than five thousand students spread among nearly a hundred mostly parochial schools; this school year [2007–08], roughly twenty thousand Milwaukee students attend 122 voucher schools. In 1996, Cleveland launched a voucher program for several thousand students, which was approved by the U.S. Supreme Court in 2002. The Florida legislature enacted a school voucher plan in 1999, as did Colorado in 2003, and the U.S. Congress, for Washington, D.C., in 2004. And although the No Child Left Behind Act rankled many conservatives because it extended the federal government's reach into a traditionally state and local realm, the [George W.] Bush administration attempted to mollify the right by including provisions that allowed failing public schools to be reconstituted by private contractors. By casting liberal opponents of vouchers as defenders of a miserable status quo in America's cities, conservatives were generally successful at portraying themselves as the genuine reformers fighting to liberate poor minority children trapped in lousy schools.

## Skepticism Tempers Enthusiasm

But in recent months, almost unnoticed by the mainstream media, the school voucher movement has abruptly stalled. Some stalwart advocates of vouchers have either repudiated the idea entirely or considerably tempered their enthusiasm for it. Exhibit A is "School Choice Isn't Enough," an article in the winter 2008 *City Journal* (the quarterly published by the conservative Manhattan Institute) written by the former voucher proponent Sol Stern. Acknowledging that voucher programs for poor children had "hit a wall," Stern concluded: "Education reformers ought to resist unreflective support for elegant-sounding theories, derived from the study of economic activity, that don't produce verifiable results in the classroom." His conversion has triggered an intense debate in conservative circles. The center-right education scholar Chester E. Finn Jr., president of the Thomas B. Fordham Foundation and a longtime critic of public school bureaucracies and teachers unions, told the *New York Sun* that he was sympathetic to Stern's argument. In his newly published memoirs, Finn also writes of his increasing skepticism that "the market's invisible hand" produces improved performance on its own. Howard Fuller, an African American who was the superintendent of schools in Milwaukee when the voucher program was launched there, and who received substantial support from the Bradley Foundation and other conservative institutions over the years, has conceded, "It hasn't worked like we thought it would in theory."

From all appearances, then, the voucher movement may not long outlive its founder, Friedman, or its most vigorous advocate and hinder, Michael Joyce, who both died in 2006. How did one of the conservative policy world's most cherished causes crumble so quickly?

## Why School Vouchers Failed

One simple reason why voucher supporters have become disillusioned is that the programs haven't delivered on their promises. School choice advocates claimed that vouchers would have two major benefits: low-income kids rescued from dysfunctional public schools would do better in private schools; and public schools would improve, thanks to the injection of some healthy competition.

Let's start with the contention that the academic performance of low-income children would improve after they moved to private institutions. For a long time, it was absurdly difficult to find out whether this was true in the one place where vouchers had been tried over an extended period: Milwaukee. After that city's initial small-scale initiative produced ambiguous, but generally unimpressive, results (and a lot of fighting over that data), the Wisconsin legislature chose to omit testing requirements altogether when the program was significantly expanded in 1998. This February [2008], however, a group of researchers led by professors Patrick J. Wolf and John F. Witte produced the first installment of a study intended to follow how comparable groups of students in the public and private voucher schools perform over time. At least at the outset, they found no statistically significant differences in the test scores between the public and private school fourth and eighth graders for the 2006–07 school year. For the private as well as the public school students, the scores generally hovered around the 33rd percentile in other words, a typically low performance for schools with high concentrations of poverty.

In Cleveland, a similar but now completed study that followed the same students over time showed dispiriting results from that city's voucher program. Tracking the scores of students who began kindergarten in the 1997–98 school year through their sixth-grade year in 2003–04, Indiana University researchers found no significant differences in overall achievement, reading, or math scores between students who used vouchers and those who stayed in public schools, after taking into account socioeconomic differences.

## The Impact on Public Schools

What about the effect of vouchers on public schools that were forced to compete for students with private ones? Voucher supporters believed that public schools would improve for two reasons. First, school administrators, faced with diminishing funds for every child that used a voucher to transfer to a private school, would be impelled to do better. And second, because parents would be encouraged to shop for the best place for their children, they would become more involved in the school they chose and hold it to higher standards.

Neither of these pressures has had a discernible impact on public school performance. In Wisconsin, this was made starkly evident in last year's results from the National Assess-

**"School of choice."**

"Shark to fish about school of fish: School of choice," by Jonny Hawkins. www.Cartoon Stock.com.

ment of Educational Progress (NAEP), the federally sponsored gold standard of testing. Reading scores for black fourth- and eighth-grade students were the lowest of any state, and the reading achievement gap between black and white students remains the worst in the nation. Since about 70 percent of Wisconsin's black students attend Milwaukee public schools, any competition-induced improvements evidently haven't amounted to much. One study, by Harvard's Caroline M. Hoxby, a voucher advocate, purported to find test score improvements in the Milwaukee public schools most affected by the risk of losing students to private schools; but the gains may have been caused simply by the lowest-performing students moving to private schools, as Hoxby herself concedes. In any case, the Manhattan Institute's Stern points out that Hoxby's analysis, published in 2001, is outdated compared to the more comprehensive and recent NAEP results, and calls the public school performance in Milwaukee after years of voucher competition "depressing."

In the Cleveland public schools, fourth-grade math scores on the NAEP test improved significantly from 2003 to 2005, though comparable gains occurred in seven of ten other big cities without vouchers. Cleveland's fourth-grade reading test improvements were more modest, and smaller than gains in Atlanta and New York City—neither of which has a public voucher program.

Also disappointing to voucher advocates has been the discovery that the innovation of choice hasn't caused parents to become noticeably more involved in public schools. One of the strategies that the Bradley Foundation initially used to lay the groundwork for vouchers in Milwaukee was to create a think tank called the Wisconsin Policy Research Institute [WPRI], which churned out studies trashing public schools. Last October, however, WPRI produced a report on the Milwaukee voucher experience, titled "The Limits of Parent-Driven Reform," that confessed: "The report you are reading did not yield the results we hoped to find. We had expected to find a wellspring of hope that increased parental involvement in the Milwaukee Public Schools (MPS) would be the key ingredient in improving student performance." Instead, the institute found that only 10 percent of parents had been the kind of "active consumers" that would "exert market-based influence to the school system," and concluded that focusing on parental choice and involvement "cannot be seen as a substitute for substantive reforms in the hierarchy of MPS and in the classrooms throughout Milwaukee." WPRI employed questionable methodology to reach its conclusions, as it had often done in the past, but this time the results undercut an initiative the institute had championed for years.

## Voucher Programs Prove Critics Right

Ultimately, the voucher experiments confirmed what their critics had asserted all along. The heart of the problem with our urban schools is neither the education bureaucracies nor teachers unions, as Chubb, Moe, and many other voucher advocates have contended, flawed though those institutions may be. Instead, as the sociologist James S. Coleman found in the 1960s, a student's family's income and the collective social and economic background of his classmates are by far the most important influences on his academic future. Not only do lower-income students tend to score relatively poorly, children of any background who attend high-poverty schools are far more likely to produce worse test results than they would in schools with primarily middle-class students. America's urban school systems remain almost universally dysfunctional, primarily because the country as a whole is about as segregated by race and income as at any time since the civil rights revolution.

This means that in the existing voucher programs, which have been confined to city school districts, students have had only a limited choice between public schools in low-income neighborhoods and private institutions—mostly parochial schools—that serve almost identical populations. In 2005, a team of reporters from the *Milwaukee Journal Sentinel* visited all but a handful of the private choice schools, and found that "the voucher schools feel, and look, surprisingly like schools in the Milwaukee Public Schools district. Both ... are struggling in the same battle to educate low-income, minority students." The *Journal Sentinel* also reported that the absence of oversight from the much-derided government bureaucracy had led to a significant waste of public funds, and even outright fraud. At least ten of the 125 private schools in the voucher program "appeared to lack the ability, resources, knowledge, or will to offer children even a mediocre education." Most of those schools were led by individuals who had negligible experience and had no resources other than state payments. (One notorious case was Alex's Academics of Excellence, a school started by a convicted rapist that continued to enroll students for years after enduring two evictions, allegations of drug use by school staff on school grounds, and an investigation by the district attorney, before finally closing in 2004.) The *Journal Sentinel* also found that many parents left their children in bad schools long after it was clear that they were failing. Recently, national studies of NAEP tests have confirmed that private and charter schools on average perform little or no better than traditional public schools (and in some cases worse), after taking into account the socioeconomic background of the students.

## Voucher Advocates Face Opposition

Vouchers would hardly be the first conservative policy fixation to founder on the shoals of empirical evidence. Yet the conservative backers of, say, supply-side economics or health savings accounts haven't traditionally allowed hard facts to deter them. Many of the erstwhile champions of school choice are having second thoughts not only because vouchers are a policy failure, but also because they didn't materialize into the political game changer that right-wing activists were hoping for.

In 1997, the conservative writer Michael Gerson (who would go on to be George W. Bush's chief speechwriter) took a tour of small-town Indiana when the state was considering a voucher program. He found that its predominantly conservative population prized its public schools (mostly because of their proud basketball tradition) and resented the suggestion that these institutions were failing their students. Over the years, various proposals for vouchers in Indiana have never progressed very far. "Conservative politicians running in this state quickly find that criticizing public education—or suggesting that some people might want to opt out—is like spitting one the school colors," Gerson wrote in *U.S. News & World Report,* noting that in 1997, support for voucher programs was higher in the liberal Northeast than the more conservative Midwest.

## Results at the Ballot Box

In 2000, both California and Michigan offered referendums on voucher programs for all children in the state. The initiatives were defeated by margins of forty-two and thirty-eight points, respectively. Voucher supporters like to blame the defeats on well-funded teachers unions, but the law professors James E. Ryan and Michael Heise found that voucher supporters had outspent the opposition in Michigan, and both sides had spent about the same amount of money in California. They concluded that the decisive resistance to vouchers had come from suburban voters who feared that the programs would take money away from local schools and worried about the arrival of lower-income and minority students in their children's classrooms. And last year [2007], in the conservative, predominantly white state of Utah, the Republican legislature put a November referendum for a voucher program on the state ballot, which Overstock.com CEO Patrick Byrne and his family supported with about $4 million. It lost by 62 percent to 38 percent—the eighth decisive loss for a statewide voucher ballot initiative. There have not been any victories.

Bill Burrow, the associate director of the Office on Competitiveness under the first President Bush, has noted that school choice is "popular in the national headquarters of the Republican Party but is unpopular among the Republican rank-and-file voters who have moved away from the inner city in part so that their children will not have to attend schools that are racially or socioeconomically integrated." Indeed, the term "voucher" has become so politically unattractive that in his January State of the Union address this year, President George W. Bush concocted the euphemism "Pell Grants for Kids" to propose a federal initiative to support private religious schools that has no chance of passing Congress.

## Results in the Courtroom

Finally, conservative activists are increasingly realizing that even if they can overcome political resistance to statewide voucher programs, they may be defeated in the end by the courts. In 2004, Colorado's supreme court ruled that the state's voucher law violated the state constitution's requirement that local districts retain control over locally raised funds. In 2006, the Florida Supreme Court struck down its statewide voucher program on the grounds that it violated a section of the constitution requiring a free and "uniform" system of public schools. Many other state constitutions include so-called Blaine Amendments, which explicitly bar government aid to sectarian schools and institutions—greatly limiting the jurisdictions in which voucher plans are legally viable.

As these realities have set in, the conservative movement's formidable resources and energy have, to a large extent, shifted away from vouchers and toward the much less controversial idea of charter schools. (Because charters are sanctioned by state governments but allowed to operate autonomously from the public school hierarchy, they appeal to the right's desire to sideline the bureaucracy and the teachers unions, while posing much less of a threat to the public schools than vouchers.) The right's spending on educational issues is now led by the Walton Family Foundation, which devoted about 80 percent of its education spending toward activities related to charter schools—an allocation of some $50 million a year. The Olin Foundation spent itself out of existence in 2005, but the Bradley Foundation remains active, with, for example, a $3 million grant in 2007 to the Charter School Growth Fund. For all the Sturm und Drang [high drama] created by the right-wing marketing machine, the number of students who have used publicly financed vouchers to attend private schools over the past eighteen years amounts to no more than the population of a medium-size suburb, and only a small fraction of those now enrolled in charter schools.

## School Vouchers Spark Innovation

The conservative infatuation with vouchers did contribute to one genuine accomplishment. The past thirty years have been a period of enormous innovation in American education. In addition to charter schools, all kinds of strategies have taken root: public school choice, new approaches to standards and accountability, magnet schools, and open enrollment plans that allow low-income city kids to attend suburban public schools and participate in various curriculum-based experiments. To the extent that the threat of vouchers represented a "nuclear option" that educators would do anything to avoid, the voucher movement helped to prompt broader but less drastic reforms that offer parents and students greater educational choices.

Along the way, some success stories have emerged, along with the many disappointments. But among the most promising approaches, as my Century Foundation colleague Richard Kahlenberg recently wrote in *Democracy*, are strategies that combine school choice initiatives like magnet and charter schools with policies to integrate poor and middle-class students. Wake County, North Carolina, for instance, introduced a policy in 2000 mandating that no school could have more than 40 percent of its students eligible for free or reduced-price lunches. Because this program makes use of choice and incentives like magnet schools to integrate poor and middle-class kids, it avoids the political hazards of compulsory busing. So far, the results have been impressive. In 2006, 60.5 percent of low-income students in Wake County passed the high school End of Course exams, compared to 43 percent of low-income students in a nearby county of a comparable size.

Of course, the inherent limit to this idea is that many urban school districts are so uniformly poor that there are few, if any, middle-class communities with schools that low-income kids can attend. One way to get around this problem would be to amend the No Child Left Behind Act to give students in failing schools the ability to attend a school outside their own district. If voucher proponents are truly motivated by a desire to help disadvantaged kids, and not merely an ideological urge to weaken public institutions, they have a chance to show it by putting their prodigious energies and money behind choice programs like these that actually work.

> *"Conventional schools offer the 50-million-plus kids who attend them the same one-size-fits-all education. This is no longer tolerable."*

# Charter Schools Are a Worthy Investment in Education

## Ron Wolk

*Ron Wolk is the founder and former editor of* Education Week *and is the chairman of Big Picture Learning. In the following viewpoint, Wolk refutes several charges against the growing charter school movement, asserting that charter schools offer innovation and motivated parents who support their children's educational goals. Wolk contends that charter schools are worthwhile because they provide a diverse range of educational opportunities.*

As you read, consider the following questions:

1. According to the author, what is one of the main justifications for charter schools?

2. How does the author rebut the charge that charter schools will destroy public schools?

Ron Wolk, "Charter Schools: An Antidote to One-Size-Fits-All Education," *Los Angeles Times*, March 23, 2010. Copyright © 2010 by Ron Wolk. For more work by Ron Wolk, try his latest book: *Wasting Minds: Why Our Education System Is Failing and What We Can Do About It*, published by ASCD. All rights reserved. Reproduced by permission.

3. According to the author, what happens to public funding when a student chooses to go to a charter school?

Education historian Diane Ravitch is half right.

In her March 14 [2010 *Los Angeles*] *Times* Op-Ed article, "The Big Idea—it's bad education policy," Ravitch warns that there is no silver-bullet solution to our education problems.

She is correct.

Having been an ardent supporter of the standards-based accountability strategy of the last 25 years and a champion of school choice, she has seen the light and become a convert, like St. Paul on the road to Damascus.

Specifically, one big idea Ravitch once supported but now denounces is our national test-driven approach to school improvement, recognizing that it is harmful to schools, to kids and to teachers.

Again, she is correct.

The other big idea she once championed but now rejects is school choice, saying it is a fad and won't work.

She is wrong.

The evidence that our overemphasis on testing is not improving schools and is actually having a negative effect is so persuasive that Ravitch doesn't elaborate on it in her column. But she does make a case against evaluating teachers on the basis of their students' test scores. That, of course, is a logical result of our obsession with testing that she has helped fuel for decades.

It should be apparent to those who make education policy that students' test scores are influenced by much more than teachers. If we really want better educators, we should change teacher preparation programs to include much more clinical experience. We also should improve teachers' working conditions and share our leadership roles with them as professionals, not union members.

## Charter vs. Traditional Public Schools in NYC

*This chart shows the number and percentage of New York City eighth graders of various ethnicities who were accepted into the city's "specialized" high schools. Among African-American and Hispanic students, a higher percentage of charter school students were offered a seat at such high schools than those who attended traditional public schools.*

### CHARTER SCHOOLS

|  | 8th Grade Enrollment | Offered Seat | % Offered Seat |
|---|---|---|---|
| African-American | 850 | 20 | 2.4% |
| Hispanic | 469 | 14 | 3.0% |
| Asian | 31 | 6 | 19.4% |
| White | 33 | 1 | 3.0% |
| TOTAL | 1,383 | 41 | 3.0% |

### TRADITIONAL PUBLIC SCHOOLS

|  | | | |
|---|---|---|---|
| African-American | 20,387 | 314 | 1.5% |
| Hispanic | 25,852 | 396 | 1.5% |
| Asian | 9,970 | 2,313 | 23.2% |
| White | 9,141 | 1,261 | 13.8% |
| TOTAL | 66,350 | 4,284 | 6.6% |

TAKEN FROM: Marcus A. Winters, "For Minorities, a Charter School Boost," *NY Post*, April 27, 2010.

# Criticizing School Choice

Ravitch devotes much of her article to criticizing choice and, particularly, charter schools. Her arguments are not new:

*Charter schools are no better than public schools and aren't really improving student achievement.*

First of all, she obviously knows that charter schools are public schools that receive public monies. It is misleading to suggest, as Ravitch does, that district schools are public but charters are not.

Second, Ravitch cites research that relies soley on test scores as a measure of success. If "test-driven" reform is unacceptable, why should test scores be a reliable basis for judging charter schools?

One of the main justifications for charters is that they offer an alternative to conventional schools and encourage innovation and experimentation. Charters often do not mirror traditional public schools in their curriculum or standard 50-minute classes.

Researchers who compare conventional schools to charter schools might just as well compare one-story schools to two-story schools. Chartering is a form of governance that allows schools to be different. What matters is not the way schools are governed but what happens inside them.

## The Role of Parents

*Charter schools get better students because parents who apply obviously care more about their children's education.*

Again, Ravitch's argument is strange. Don't we want parents to care about their kids' education? She also says charters admit by lottery and "counsel out" unwanted students; "public" schools, on the other hand, have to take all comers, including the students charters don't want.

Charter schools are public schools and are therefore required to accept all students on a first-come, first-serve basis. They resort to lotteries when demand exceeds supply, which is better and fairer than following the example of private schools and colleges. She points to the widely publicized schools run by the Knowledge is Power Program [KIPP] as evidence of "counseling out." Interestingly, KIPP schools are charter schools that are essentially traditional schools on steroids.

Ravitch cites studies in Boston, Washington, New York and Houston showing that district schools end up with a disproportionate share of the hardest to educate students. I haven't seen the study, but its conclusions don't surprise me. The student bodies in many big-city schools are made up almost entirely of poor and minority kids. For various reasons, the parents of those kids send them to the neighborhood schools without regard to educational quality. Charters attract students who are dissatisfied with conventional schools.

## The Effect on Public Schools

*Charter schools will undermine (Ravich says "destroy") public education by luring students and draining funds that would otherwise go to conventional district schools.*

I repeat: Charter schools are as much a part of "public education" as any other public school. If they undermine anything, it's the bad schools entrenched in the system.

Students who choose a charter school do take their state funding with them. That is the way the system works. The migration of students to charter schools is no different than the migration of students to suburban schools. Affluent parents have long had school choice because they could afford more expensive homes, which is really the "tuition" for attending a suburban school.

Ravitch criticizes the notion of competition and "free market" forces that are often cited to justify charters. I'm with her on that. There is little evidence that those forces, if they really exist, have made much of a dent on the larger system.

But choice is less about competition than it is about providing a diversity of educational opportunities for the most diverse student body in American history. Conventional schools offer the 50-million-plus kids who attend them the same one-size-fits-all education. This is no longer tolerable.

> *"If our goal is to improve education for all students, the bulk of the evidence suggests that market-based education reforms, including charter schools, are not going to help us achieve it."*

# Charter Schools Are No Better than Public Schools

## William G. Wraga

*William G. Wraga is a professor in the University of Georgia College of Education's Department of Lifelong Education, Administration, and Policy. In the following viewpoint, he finds that charter school policies have often been hijacked by free-market advocates who want to privatize public schools. Wraga also points out that charter school students perform no better than public school students overall.*

As you read, consider the following questions:

1. According to Wraga, what was the reasoning behind the idea for charter schools in the 1980s?

2. What three interest groups does the author say have influenced charter school policy and practice?

3. According to the author, what has international research on charter schools in the United Kingdom and New Zealand shown?

The original intent of charter schools, to increase the professional autonomy of teachers so they could explore innovative ways to educate children and youth, has given way to other agendas that have grafted onto the movement.

Increasingly, charter school policies have been influenced by market ideology that treats the movement as a vehicle for privatizing public schools.

Research reveals that, in practice, charter school "innovations" too often occur more on the management side than on the educational side of schooling.

And despite anecdotal reports of local successes, overall, charter school students perform no better than non-charter public school students.

## The Focus Shifts to the Classroom

To improve the education of all students, policy-makers should focus not on the governance structures of schools, but on the improvement of curriculum and instruction in classrooms.

The idea for charter schools emerged in the late 1980s as a way to enhance professional autonomy of teachers that would empower them to identify ways to educate students that were more effective than what the existing bureaucracy would allow.

Since that time, charter schools have enjoyed support from a wide range of interests, including teacher unions, minority rights advocates, and advocates of deregulation and free market reforms.

Over time, the agendas of these different interest groups have influenced charter school policy and practice.

"Excuses, Excuses, Excuses," by Jerry King, copyright FNO Press. nochildleft.com.

## Questioning Conventional Wisdom

Today, the rhetoric supporting charter schools usually emphasizes an offer of autonomy in return for accountability for educators and increased choice for parents.

Because the main idea behind charter schools is that exemption from cumbersome state regulations will free local educators to generate more effective ways to educate students, one might expect that local reports of charter school success would identify the regulations that previously had impeded school performance.

Armed with this information, policy-makers could abolish those regulations so that all public schools would benefit.

Moreover, if cumbersome regulations are really the principal obstacle to school improvement, as the case for charter schools implies, then why not simply waive these cumbersome regulations for all public schools?

Not only would such a policy free all public schools to pursue innovative solutions to their educational problems, but also the time, energy and money spent on preparing tedious charter petitions, then negotiating the petition process could be invested directly in local school improvement.

## The Push for Privatization

Neither of these things are likely to happen because, despite the appealing rhetoric about autonomy and choice, another agenda has quietly come to reshape charter school policies: namely, to impose market-based reforms on the public school system in order to prepare it eventually for privatization.

Although the federal No Child Left Behind Act and the Georgia Charter School Act currently require all charter schools to be public, that is, funded by public money, both laws allow the public money to be paid to private for-profit companies to run charter schools.

This legislation has opened the door wider for privatization of public schools.

Research into charter school practice has found that "innovations" that charter schools typically implement have more to do with management and advertising than with curriculum and instruction.

Classroom practices in charter schools are little different than classroom practices in non-charter public schools.

## Promises Have Gone Unfulfilled

The promise that the deregulated governance structures of charter schools would precipitate the introduction of new and more effective classroom practices remains unfulfilled.

When charter schools and other market-based reforms for public education were first proposed, there was no evidence that they would actually improve education.

Now that these reforms have been attempted, the evidence is still not in their favor.

Overall, the available evidence indicates that, nationally, charter schools do not outperform non-charter public schools in terms of improved academic achievement of students.

And international research has found that countries such as the United Kingdom, New Zealand and the United States that have implemented market-based school reforms, such as school choice and charter schools, have higher levels of educational inequality in terms of academic achievement of students.

Countries such as Denmark, Sweden and Japan that have strong publicly supported school systems and few, if any, market-based educational experiments, enjoy high levels of both access to education and academic achievement.

## Finding Reforms That Work

If our goal is to improve education for all students, the bulk of the evidence suggests that market-based education reforms, including charter schools, are not going to help us achieve it.

The best policy for improving public schools is to invest directly in reforms that have been proven to work.

Those reforms should focus not on the business side of schools, but on implementing classroom practices that have been demonstrated to improve curriculum, instruction and assessment—and ultimately student learning.

> *"You'll find that the D.C. program pro-vides a model that can work well in other communities around our nation."*

# The D.C. Opportunity Scholarship Program Should Continue

## Targeted News Service

*Targeted News Service is a newswire with one of the world's largest collections of government-oriented information. In the following viewpoint, House Speaker John Boehner supports re-newing the legislation for the D.C. Opportunity Scholarship. Boehner believes that the competition caused by the program will raise the bar as "competition makes everybody better." He presents the views and opinions of beneficiaries from the pro-gram as support for the legislation's renewal, asking that the House support the program and give others the same chance for success.*

As you read, consider the following questions:

1. What does Boehner believe to be a way to protect the American Dream as stated in the article?

Targeted News Service, "Speaker Boehner Calls for House to Renew D.C. School Choice Program," March 30, 2011. Reproduced by permission.

2. According to Boehner, how does the education establishment in the United States view the D.C. Opportunity Scholarship?

3. Who does Boehner claim are the program's "greatest ambassadors"?

House Speaker John Boehner, R-Ohio, issued the following news release:

House Speaker John Boehner (R-OH) today [March 30, 2011] spoke on the House floor in support of H.R. 471, legislation renewing the bipartisan, successful D.C. Opportunity Scholarship Program, which has helped thousands of disadvantaged students gain access to a quality education. Boehner also submitted for the record letters from a parent and several students who hope the [Barack] Obama Administration will work with Congress to ensure the program will continue....

"Let me start out by thanking the members of the Oversight and Government Reform Committee for their work on this bill. Thank you also to our 50 co-sponsors and all the members on both sides who are standing with us today. I appreciate the efforts of our colleagues in the Senate ... particularly [Connecticut Senator] Joe Lieberman ... who are working on similar legislation.

"Today, the House will have the opportunity to do something special for the future of our country. I think just about every member would agree we have work to do when it comes to our education system. Americans are concerned that their children won't be able to have the same blessings they've had. And if we want to protect the American Dream, there's no substitute for a quality education.

"My view's always been, education reform starts with giving children in need a way out of our most underachieving public schools. Of course, that doesn't mean that we abandon those schools. It means we take some of the pressure off of them while they work to turn themselves around. So we came

## Benefits of the D.C. Opportunity Scholarship Program

- Students who used their opportunity scholarships had a 21% higher graduation rate than students who were not offered scholarships, and participating OSP [D.C. Opportunity Scholarship Program] students continue to show academic gain.

- The U.S. Department of Education's (DOE) Institute for Education Sciences found that OSP participants' gains were the largest achievement impact of any of the 11 programs studied so far. DOE's own "What Works Clearinghouse" has validated the research behind the OSP.

- Four consecutive studies from Georgetown University and the University of Arkansas found that parents are very satisfied, more involved in their children's education, and becoming savvy educational consumers.

*"D.C. Opportunity Scholarship Program,"*
*www.SaveSchoolChoice.com, June 2010.*

together here about seven years ago and said, let's try something different. Instead of just throwing money at the problem, let's empower parents from lower-income families to choose the schools that are best for them. We wouldn't deny any school money that they'd already been receiving—we would just be injecting freedom and competition into a system caught up in the status quo.

"And we had a strong bipartisan coalition, including: Anthony Williams, who was the mayor here [Washington, D.C.] at the time, and [Texas representative] Dick Armey, who for years led this fight in the House, paving the way for this program. He and I started working together on school choice in the early 1990s when we served on the Education and Labor Committee. We said, let's give these kids in our capital city a real chance at success and a real shot at the American Dream that they don't have. What do we have to be afraid of? Well, as it turned out, there was nothing to be afraid of. Thousands of families have taken advantage of the D.C. Opportunity Scholarship Program. And there's strong evidence that it's both effective and cost effective.

"Unfortunately, the education establishment in our country sees this Opportunity Scholarship Program as a threat. In reality, this is an opportunity to raise the bar, because competition makes everybody better. I think if you look beyond the talking points and focus on the facts, you'll find that the D.C. program provides a model that can work well in other communities around our nation.

"Now, this issue is important to me—but I'll tell you this: this is not about me. I'm proud to say I've supported the Opportunity Scholarship Program from the get-go, but I'm even more proud of the fact I had nothing to do with its success. For that, we can thank the students and the parents who have become more than just the program's beneficiaries—they are its greatest ambassadors. In recent days, I've received letters from many of them asking Congress to do the right thing, and I'll be submitting some of those for the record.

"You see, they know what it was like before. They remember living just blocks from these great schools, but feeling miles away from them. All they ask us to do is help ensure others get the same chance they've had. That's no controversial idea—it's just the American way. So if we're serious about bipartisan education reform, we should start by saving this successful, bipartisan program that has helped so many underprivileged children get a quality education. I urge the House to support and save this important program."

> *"Over its short life, the [D.C. Opportu-*
> *nity Scholarship] program proved al-*
> *most entirely ineffective."*

# The D.C. Opportunity Scholarship Program Should Be Terminated

## Alex Koppelman

*Alex Koppelman is a staff writer for Salon.com. In the following viewpoint, he asserts that the D.C. Opportunity Scholarship Program was ineffective at getting students out of the worst schools and into better ones. Koppelman also notes that studies show that there was no academic benefit to the program, because students receiving vouchers performed the same as students without them.*

As you read, consider the following questions:

1. How many Washington, D.C., students receive scholarships from the D.C. Opportunity Scholarship Program?

2. According to a 2007 Government Accountability Office (GAO) report, as cited by Koppelman, how many schools in the program indicated that half of their teachers did not have at least a bachelor's degree in the 2004–2005 school year?

3. According to the GAO as cited by Koppelman, what percentage of scholarship users attended schools with tuitions less than the $7,500 cap?

The federally funded program that provides about 1,700 Washington, D.C. school children with up to $7,500 in vouchers to attend private school may have just gotten its death blow.

## A Political Controversy

A provision in the omnibus spending bill that passed the Senate Tuesday evening [March 10, 2009] requires re-approval of the program in order to extend it beyond the next school year. Sen. John Ensign, R-Nev., had offered an amendment to strip that language from the legislation, but on Tuesday, the Senate voted Ensign's proposal down, 50-39. As Democrats generally oppose school vouchers, the GOP fears—probably correctly— that this will mean the end of the program, as an extension likely wouldn't be able to pass when it comes up for a vote, if it's even allowed to go that far.

"In drafting this bill, Democrats put their political agenda ahead of educating our children. As a result, students who chose to leave a failing school and attend a better, safer school will have to return to the school they decided to leave," Ensign said in a statement. "This is such a tragic situation."

Ensign wasn't the only one bemoaning the potential end of the program. There's been a firestorm of criticism on the right over the issue, and people from other parts of the political spectrum have been advocating for the funding as well. Even President Obama's secretary of education, Arne Duncan, gave D.C. vouchers his limited blessing recently, saying that [although] he opposes the idea generally, kids already in private schools because of the program should be allowed to remain.

## The Truth About the Program

But by all appearances, this experiment in school vouchers really should be allowed to die. Over its short life, the program proved almost entirely ineffective. Actually, its only real success was as a stimulus for D.C.'s beleaguered Catholic schools—they, not the students, proved to be the vouchers' biggest beneficiaries.

Obviously, there can be some benefit—even just an emotional one, rather than something that can be measured—to getting out of one of D.C.'s public schools, which can be a bad environment, and into a better one. But that assumes the students were getting out of the worst schools and into appreciably better ones, and that wasn't always the case. (In fact, kids who attended the city's worst schools were proportionally less likely to receive vouchers.) Moreover, when it came to academic performance, studies repeatedly showed no significant effect. The RAND Corporation summarized the Department of Education's first impact study of the program this way:

> Because the program was oversubscribed, scholarships were awarded by lottery. To examine total program impact on student achievement, the study compared the results of lottery winners with those of lottery losers (regardless of whether the winners actually used their scholarships or whether the losers attended public schools). The authors found no impact, positive or negative, on average test scores in reading or math. Similarly, they found no impact of the effect of using a voucher to attend a private school on average reading or math test scores.

On top of that, the program was poorly run; it lacked proper oversight, and had some fairly obvious, and quite serious, flaws. Those were exposed in a 2007 report by the Government Accountability Office [GAO], which savaged the voucher system generally, along with the Washington scholarship Fund (WSF), which administered it. Among other problems, the GAO found that, in the 2004–2005 school year, "at least 3 of 52 schools that participated that year indicated that at least half of their teachers did not have at least a bachelor's degree, and 6 schools indicated that about 10 to 20 percent of their teachers lacked at least a bachelor's degree. Further, many of the schools were not accredited, and there is no evidence that they submitted evidence of educational soundness."

This would have been more forgivable if WSF hadn't provided parents with incomplete—sometimes even inaccurate—information about the schools to which they could apply. Because of this failure, the GAO concluded, "parents might have used opportunity scholarships to place their children in private schools that were *less successful in raising achievement levels than the public schools their children previously attended.*" (My emphasis.)

## The Surprising Irony

Considering that voucher advocates often use "school choice" as their preferred term, the D.C. experience was tinged with a particularly bitter irony: Participating students had few options when picking the school they wanted to attend. "Some students who received scholarships had limited choices, particularly students in the upper grades and those who wanted to attend a secular school," the GAO report said. "For example, according to WSF data for school year 2005–2006, only about 70 openings were available at the high school level (compared to about 650 for students in kindergarten through grade 5 and about 200 for students in grades 6–8). The majority of scholarship students attending high schools went to one religious school. . . . In addition, students who desired a secular school had a limited number to choose from, since most of the participating private schools were Catholic or Protestant, and these schools offered most of the openings."

Republicans have criticized people like President [Barack] Obama and Sen. Dick Durbin, D-Ill., who proposed the spending bill's voucher-killing language, for sending their children to private schools while voting against giving the same choice to other parents. There maybe some validity to that argument, or at least an emotional appeal, especially because there are two students who receive vouchers who go to Sidwell Friends, the school Obama's children attend. But those kids are the exception, not the rule; for the most part, the GAO found, voucher recipients didn't get to go to schools like Sidwell that fall on the higher end of the tuition range.

"About 88 percent of all scholarship users attended schools with tuitions below the $7,500 cap," the GAO said. "Although tuition rates varied, only 3 percent attended the most expensive schools that charged $20,000 or more."

> "Racially diverse schools are associated
> with achievement in math and reading
> for Latino and African-American stu-
> dents."

# Diverse Magnet Schools Improve Access to Education

*Susan Eaton*

*Susan Eaton is an author and the research director at the Charles Hamilton Houston Institute at Harvard Law School. In the following viewpoint, she points out that the example of magnet schools in Hartford, Connecticut, shows that such schools succeed in creating pockets of racially and economically diverse educational institutions and that students attending magnet schools achieve a better academic performance than non-magnet school students. Eaton finds that charter schools are often favored over magnet schools, despite the better record of academic achievement for magnet schools.*

As you read, consider the following questions:

1. According to the author, why did magnet schools start in Connecticut?

Susan Eaton, "The Pull of Magnets," *The Nation*, June 14, 2010. Copyright © 2010 by The Nation. All rights reserved. Reproduced by permission.

2. How much does the author claim the Department of Education will spend to promote school choice, according to its 2011 budget?

3. According to Magnet Schools of America, as cited by Eaton, how many magnet schools are there in the United States?

Just beyond the bodegas painted in tropical hues, past the bleak jail for juveniles and the vacancy signs along Broad Street in Hartford, Connecticut, a startlingly sleek, sterile collection of buildings materializes. Weekday mornings, a chain of yellow buses encircles the compound. Under the eyes of security guards and cameras, kids hop down, saunter into buildings and settle into classrooms where the mix of complexions and family incomes does not match Census data culled from these streets.

Many of the children scattered among the elementary, middle and two high schools have indeed been "bused" in, to engineer the creation of racially and economically diverse schools in this otherwise extremely poor, sharply segregated Latino neighborhood. Some of the children who attend the schools in this "learning corridor" live nearby. Others come from the African-American neighborhoods to the north, and a large share travel up to an hour from the lily-white suburbs that surround the city of Hartford, where 46 percent of children are poor. Several other "magnet" schools in and around the city open their doors each morning to a student body that reflects the diversity of the region, as opposed to the homogeneity found in schools that enroll kids from just one town or neighborhood.

"It has been nothing short of a beautiful experience," says Mara Whitman, a white mother of four who opted for a magnet in Hartford over the far more affluent and far less diverse schools in her town, West Hartford. "To be honest, it was not the diversity that attracted us. It was the educational program.

The theories that drove instruction were well thought, based in evidence. . . . But it wasn't long before we realized that the diversity made the experience rich."

## The Potential of Magnet Schools

After a state court ruled in 1996 that the region's public schools were segregated, in violation of Connecticut's Constitution, magnet schools became the principal remedy. Urban and suburban parents alike were quick to sign their children up for the new schools, which were often (though not always) located in urban communities of color. The waiting lists grew long for the more successful schools. Thanks to an unyielding push by civil rights lawyers, state legislators went on to approve funding for more magnets. Now, in one of the nation's most segregated and economically stratified regions, tiny centers of racial and economic integration have taken root. Significantly—like students attending magnet schools in California, Nevada, Florida, Illinois and other areas—children in Connecticut's magnet schools have registered promising academic results, often outdoing those in traditional public schools, which were, by comparison, sharply segregated by race and class. This past December, a study in the peer-reviewed journal *Educational Evaluation and Policy Analysis* compared academic results between students who'd applied to Connecticut's magnets and were not selected through the blind lottery and students who were selected and got to attend a magnet school. The magnet school students who lived in urban ZIP codes (these students are mostly Latino or black) made greater gains in math and reading than did their fellow students who stayed in the urban (segregated) schools. What's more, the suburban students—this group is largely white—attending magnets outdid their peers at traditional suburban (and generally much whiter) schools, too. The "achievement gap" between white students and students of color tended to be smaller in Connecticut's magnet schools than it was in traditional schools.

While research on magnets and academic achievement is far from conclusive and often complicated by methodological concerns, you might think that the increasingly promising results emerging from a variety of locations, coupled with magnets' desegregation mission, would make them serious contenders for the $4.3 billion made available through the Education Department's competitive grant program, Race to the Top. But the [Barack] Obama administration's reform strategy mostly overlooks the nation's thousands of magnet schools. Instead, administration officials much more strongly favor a newer "reform"—charter schools, which demonstrate no evidence of sustained, large-scale success and tend to compound racial and economic segregation.

## Charter Versus Magnet Schools

Charter schools are similar to magnet schools in that students choose to attend them, and the schools usually offer a specialized theme or curricular strength, such as visual arts or science. But magnets, begun in the 1960s and expanded in the '80s as voluntary desegregation measures, are operated by public schools or publicly funded agencies that work closely with public schools. They are thus subject to all the regulations (and union rules and civil rights protections) associated with public schools. Though some magnets have clearly strayed from their original desegregation mission, the magnet schools that operate as originally intended either attract a racially diverse student body or are at least actively trying to. They usually provide free public transportation for students to travel longer than typical distances. Charter schools, on the other hand, can be operated by just about anyone, including private corporations, nonprofits, individuals who may or may not have experience with teaching children or operating an educational institution, or religious groups in partnership with other entities. They don't necessarily need to offer free transportation, and they are under no mandates to be racially or economically diverse.

Charter schools have enjoyed enthusiastic rhetorical support since Obama's presidential campaign and, in recent months, increasing monetary support. In March 2009, the president told the US Hispanic Chamber of Commerce: "I call on states to reform their charter rules and lift caps on the number of allowable charter schools wherever such caps are in place." In public statements about Race to the Top, Education Secretary Arne Duncan made it clear that states that limit charter school expansion would not be looked upon favorably in Race to the Top's competitive grant program.

Lawmakers in several states, strapped for cash mid-recession, either did or at least tried to do exactly what the administration told them to do. Some did it fast, passing laws that supported the development of more charters, without evidence that such schools were consistently doing well by children. In response to the administration's pressure, Louisiana, Massachusetts, Illinois, Tennessee and Delaware either lifted their caps on charter schools or let their moratoriums lapse. And not surprisingly, the winners in the first round of funding, announced at the end of this past March, were Delaware and Tennessee, where officials had significantly loosened restrictions on how many charter schools could operate. In Tennessee, legislators had even created a new funding stream to pay for charter school facilities. Together, the two states will receive about $600 million, not only for charters, of course, but for larger reform plans in which charters play an important role.

## Charter Schools Get the Funding

The Education Department's proposed 2011 budget would spend $490 million to promote school choice, the vast majority of which would go toward charter schools. This amounts to a 20 percent increase—or about $81 million—over what charters receive in the current budget. By comparison, federal funding for magnet schools comes mainly through the Magnet Schools Assistance Program [MSAP]. This year, MSAP will provide about $100 million to some forty schools across the country. The program, though, has been flat-funded since 2008. President Obama's proposed 2011 budget does include a modest funding increase for the program, bringing it up to $110 million.

"The federal government is beginning to pay us a little bit more attention," says Robert Brooks, executive director of the Washington-based Magnet Schools of America, which sponsors conferences and provides technical services to magnet schools. "But this overemphasis on charter schools is astonishing. Magnet schools have a much longer record of success in terms of academic achievement and equity. I think maybe the difference is that charter schools are viewed as a newer concept. People tend to like the idea of a newer concept. Legislators especially like to be associated with newer concepts."

Magnets, Brooks supposes, are unfairly suffering from their roots as "equity-minded institutions from the '70s that sought integration." Now, he adds, "there are all kinds of people questioning whether that's even a valid way to educate children anymore, which flies in the face of what the research says. But we are not straying from our message: diversity is beneficial for kids and for society."

## Addressing the Disparity

The charter/magnet imbalance has unnerved many advocates, who are urging federal officials to give the well-performing, racially diverse magnet schools consideration at least equal to charters. (Full disclosure: the Harvard-based Institute where I work is a member of the National Coalition on School Diversity, which has submitted formal comment letters to the administration on related issues.)

"We think that the practice of ignoring magnet school successes and pushing charters as the only major focus of choice in federal initiatives . . . ignores some strong evidence about [magnets'] benefits," Professor Gary Orfield, co-director of UCLA's Civil Rights Project, wrote in a 2009 memo to top Education Department officials. "In thinking about school choice and innovation we recommend that . . . increases in resources be competitively available between both options, and that civil rights policies common in magnets be extended to charters."

The Civil Rights Project released a study in January demonstrating that charter schools tend to exacerbate segregation, which is linked to a host of short- and long-term educational and social inequalities. African-Americans, our most segregated racial group, are the students most segregated in charter schools. According to the report, 70 percent of black students enrolled in charter schools attend schools that are 90 to 100 percent nonwhite. This is about twice the share of black public school students who attend schools that are segregated. What's more, the report found that charter schools failed to produce data related to enrollment and accessibility for students who are still learning English or about students from low-income families.

## The Importance of Racially Diverse Schools

Populist commentators of all ideological stripes have won easy applause in recent years by passionately insisting that when it comes to learning, demographics do not matter. They point to isolated examples of all-black or all-Latino schools—often charter schools—that "beat the odds." However, the notion that high-poverty racially segregated schools are equal to middle-class schools has been consistently disproved by a half-century of research. Loudly heralding the relative few that "beat the odds" (typically not for more than two years) ob-

# What Is a Magnet School?

A Magnet school is part of the public school system. Usually students are zoned into their schools based on location. Students mostly go to the school which they are closest to (this may not always be true since boundaries can seem arbitrary). With Magnet schools, the public school system has created schools that exist outside of zoned school boundaries. The point of them is that they usually have something special to offer over a regular school which makes attending them an attractive choice to many students, thereby increasing the diversity of the student population within them (in theory).

Magnet schools are different from private or parochial schools in that they remain part of the public school system. They differ from Charter schools in that they remain part of the public school system bureaucratically. Charter schools have a different organizational model (i.e., they have a charter that releases them from the regular school administration). Magnet schools operate under the same public school administration (they don't operate on their own).

Distinguishing them from other public schools, Magnet schools usually have alternative or otherwise compelling modes of instruction. . . . Magnet schools differ from other public schools in that they receive additional funding to enable them to spend more money on their students, supplies, teachers, programs, etc.

*Grace Chen, "What Is a Magnet School?"*
Public School Review, *December 4, 2007.*

scures the harsh reality of the odds themselves, which remain low for kids who attend high-poverty segregated schools.

The weight of social science evidence demonstrates that racially diverse schools are associated with achievement in math and reading for Latino and African-American students, with more advanced critical thinking skills, intellectual engagement and a reduction in racial stereotyping. Learning challenges that may be related to stress, poverty, health problems or neighborhood violence, researchers are starting to understand, may be more effectively overcome in schools that are not sharply segregated by race and class.

The decades of findings on these points have led to something rare in social science—a consensus. In 2007 the National Academy of Education wrote, "In summary, the research evidence supports the conclusion that the overall academic and social effects of increased racial diversity are likely to be positive. Racial diversity per se does not guarantee such positive outcomes, but it provides the necessary conditions under which other educational policies can facilitate improved academic achievement, improved intergroup relations, and positive long-term outcomes."

## The Failure of Charter Schools

Meanwhile, there is no consistent evidence and certainly no research consensus that charter schools, just by virtue of being charter schools, do any better, on average, than traditional public schools. A 2009 study conducted in Boston returned typical results. Some charters there did better than the traditional public schools, and some did worse. A study of charters in Minnesota, which has the nation's oldest system of charters, found that students in charters generally did less well on achievement tests than similar students in public schools. That study, conducted by the University of Minnesota–based Institute on Race and Poverty, also found that charter schools tended to worsen segregation levels in Minneapolis and St. Paul. Researchers concluded that "although a few charter schools perform well on standardized tests, most offer low income parents and parents of color an inferior choice—a choice between low-performing traditional public schools and charter schools that perform even worse."

A 2005 study from the Economic Policy Institute found that in Florida, Michigan, Texas and Pennsylvania, students in charter schools that had been operating for more than three years did no better on state tests than public school students did. The number of charter schools, however, has more than doubled over the past decade, from about 2,300 in 2001 to nearly 5,000 now. According to Magnet Schools of America, there are about 4,000 magnet schools in the United States, enrolling about 2.5 million students.

That charters do not upset the stratified structure of public education—i.e., they tend to leave white kids in "white" schools and African-American students in identifiable "black" schools—may be exactly what makes them, at first glance, appear politically neater than magnet schools. After all, if magnets work as intended, they absolutely will alter the status quo of entrenched residential segregation by allowing kids of differing racial backgrounds to pursue opportunity across manmade boundaries. (As even magnet advocates are quick to point out, not all magnets are racially diverse. Those that are not, diversity advocates argue, should not be the ones that are rewarded with federal dollars.)

## Magnet Schools Address Racial and Economic Inequalities

There is no sign that the administration might be open to rethinking its infatuation with charters. However, the mission of magnet schools seems to be in line with the administration's recently and clearly articulated concerns about racial segregation and concentrated poverty—creating an opening for advocates to press for magnet school funding increases beyond what the administration has already proposed.

In March, Secretary Duncan stood at the Edmund Pettus Bridge in Selma, Alabama, and reiterated a statement Barack Obama had made in Philadelphia as a presidential candidate: "Segregated schools were, and are, inferior schools. We still haven't fixed them fifty years after *Brown v. Board of Education*—and the inferior education they provided, then and now, helps explain the pervasive achievement gap between today's black and white students."

Similarly, at a Black History Month celebration recently, Housing and Urban Development Secretary Shaun Donovan stated even more clearly a commitment to reducing segregation and concentrated poverty. "The neighborhoods of concentrated poverty we see in communities across America didn't result in spite of government—but in many cases because of it," Donovan said, touting the administration's "commitment to building more inclusive communities." He added that "we expect communities receiving federal funding to end practices that limit diversity and start promoting stable, inclusive communities."

Civil rights groups view magnet schools as a potentially good offering for an "inclusion"-seeking Democratic administration to carry across the legislative aisle. Magnets embody "choice," and so should win support from conservatives who advocate free-market solutions for public schools. Magnet schools' survival hinges on their knack for "innovation," as educators must create curricular themes that attract families. As public schools, magnets are "accountable" and are judged on results from state-administered tests. Modern buzzwords apply, but at heart magnets remain civil rights–era remedies to structural inequality. Even if they aren't shiny and new, magnets might come close to that rare mix of having something for everyone.

"I hear about other schools that are all-black or all-white trying to teach about how the society is diverse and trying to get it through to kids that they have to understand other perspectives," says Lorna Shipp-Parmlee, who has three children attending magnets who ordinarily would have been assigned to high-poverty schools in their predominantly black Hartford neighborhood. "But when you are in a school that really is diverse, you aren't learning diversity—you are actually living it."

*"When educational leaders decided to create magnet schools, they didn't just get it wrong, they got it backwards."*

# Magnet Schools Are Deeply Flawed

## Victor Harbison

*Victor Harbison is a Chicago teacher. In the following viewpoint, he contends that magnet schools have pulled the best students out of neighborhood schools, depriving the students who remain of positive role models. Harbison argues that it would have been more logical to pull out the bottom ten percent of public school students to give them an education tailored to their educational needs, offering them a better chance to succeed academically.*

As you read, consider the following questions:

1. How did public schools adapt to magnet schools, according to the author?

2. Why does the author believe that adopting a business model for the educational system is bound to fail?

3. Why does the author view the argument that magnet schools are a long-term solution for education in the United States as irrational?

Given the recent economic news, it seems everyone wants to talk about the long-term impact of short-term thinking. Why not do the same with education and magnet schools? Think of the issues educators faced 30 or 40 years ago: Smart kids not being challenged? Academically under-prepared kids, most of them ethnic minorities, moving in and test scores going down? It's completely logical that they chose a path to create magnet schools. But it was a short-term solution that has had long-term negative consequences.

I take my students to lots of outside events where they are required to interact with students who come from magnet or high-performing suburban schools. What I see time after time is how my kids rise to the occasion, performing as well (or at least trying to) as those students whose test scores or geographic location landed them in much more demanding academic environments.

On a daily basis, I see the same kids who do amazing things when surrounded by their brightest counterparts from other schools slip into every negative stereotype you can imagine, and worse, when surrounded by their under-performing peers at our "neighborhood" school.

## Magnet Schools Get It Wrong

When educational leaders decided to create magnet schools, they didn't just get it wrong, they got it backwards. They pulled out the best and brightest from our communities and sent them away. The students who are part of the "great middle" now find themselves in an environment where the peers who have the greatest influence in their school are the least positive role models.

Schools adapted, and quickly. We tightened security, installed metal detectors, and adopted ideas like zero-tolerance.

And neighborhood schools, without restrictive admission policies based on test scores, quickly spiraled downward—somewhat like an economy. Except in education, we can't lay off students who have a negative impact on the school culture. That is why adopting such a business model for the educational system has been and always will be a recipe for failure.

What should have been done was to pull out the bottom ten percent. Educational leaders could have greatly expanded the alternative school model and sent struggling students to a place that had been designed to meet their educational needs. Now, hundreds of millions of dollars later, we are no closer to meeting the needs of the struggling student, but the system has created collateral damage, namely the great middle, who are forced everyday to go to class in a school that is more unchallenging, unwelcoming and dangerous than it has to be.

Imagine if pulling out the "bottom ten" had been the policy for the past 30 years. Neighborhood schools could have purred along like the go-go '90s under Clinton and the students with the greatest needs, facing the greatest challenges, would have had millions of dollars in resources devoted to their education in brand new state-of-the-art buildings (with Ivy League–educated, amazing teachers, no doubt). Just imagine.

Instead, the system as it is stratifies communities. By the time they graduate high school, many of the brightest kids already feel alienated from their neighborhoods; after all, they spend the majority of their day somewhere else.

I look forward to the arguments defending magnet schools. They are legion and many are spot on. That is, if you can live with the idea of condemning the vast majority of students in your community to substandard schools. No one can rationally argue that they are a good long-term solution to what ails schools in this country.

*"The fact is Head Start does work for a vast majority of children."*

# Head Start Is a Worthwhile Program

## Yasmina Vinci

*Yasmina Vinci is the executive director of the National Head Start Association. In the following viewpoint, she addresses critics of Head Start who point to a study that shows mixed results from the program. Vinci argues that there have been numerous long-term studies of Head Start and all reveal that the program results in key improvements in high-school graduation rates, academic performance, vocabulary levels, and emotional development.*

As you read, consider the following questions:

1. Why does Vinci believe that certain results of the recent Head Start study were inaccurate?

2. What percentage of the control group in the study were enrolled in other Head Start centers that were not part of the study at some point before they entered kindergarten, according to the author?

3. What percentage of the control group attended other preschool programs for an average of four hours per week more than Head Start students, according to the author?

A few active Head Start opponents have inaccurately portrayed the recent Head Start Impact Study [IS] as being negative to Head Start, and by doing so have unfairly misled a number of fair-minded observers. In actuality, the Study was yet another affirmation of the decades of rigorous peer-reviewed research showing that Head Start works.

The Head Start IS measured the school readiness of Head Start children compared to a control group, some of whom stayed home and many of whom attended other preschool programs. The result was dramatically favorable to the Head Start children. The prime conclusion of the study was that the Head Start children left Head Start better prepared "on every measure of children's preschool experiences measured in this study."

## A Tainted Result

The study also looked at certain measures of academic performance at the end of first grade and was unable to detect any statistically significant difference between the two groups, a fact that Head Start opponents have trumpeted loudly. What the opponents fail to mention is that the data from the control group were totally contaminated by the time children entered school.

Parents in the control group, as they should have been, were allowed to do what was best for the children—find another program not included in the study. In fact, 40 percent of the control group children were enrolled in other Head Start centers that were not a part of the study at some point before they entered kindergarten. An additional 25 percent of the

### 2009 Head Start Program Statistics

| | |
|---|---|
| **Enrollment** | **904,153** |
| **Ages** | |
| Number of 5 year olds and older | 3.0% |
| Number of 4 year olds | 51.0% |
| Number of 3 year olds | 36.0% |
| Number of under 3 years of age | 10.0% |
| **Racial/Ethnic Composition** | |
| American Indian/Alaska Native | 4.0% |
| Black/African American | 30.0% |
| White | 39.9% |
| Asian | 1.7% |
| Hawaiian/Pacific Islander | 0.6% |
| Bi-Racial/Multi-Racial | 7.8% |
| Unspecified/Other | 16.7% |
| Hispanic/Latino | 35.9% |
| **Number of Grantees** | **1,591** |
| Number of Classrooms | 49,200 |
| **Average Cost Per Child** | **$7,600** |
| **Paid Staff** | **212,000** |
| **Volunteers** | **1,274,000** |

TAKEN FROM: US Department of Health and Human Services, 2010.

control group children attended other preschool programs for an average of four hours/week more than the Head Start children spent in Head Start.

In reality, there was no longer a valid control group by the time children reached first grade. There was no attempt made by the study to compare individual children who had actually attended Head Start with those who had not.

## Head Start Benefits Students

Issues of fade-out at specific points in the education process are not new. Previous studies have shown ebbs and flows in achievement from grade to grade throughout the educational experience. In spite of the ups and downs in achievement, long-term studies continue to reach the same conclusion: Head Start results in significant improvements in a wide variety of educational outcomes and life outcomes, such as increased high school graduation rates; fewer grade repetitions; fewer kids going into special education classes; higher vocabulary levels; better emotional development; reduced mortality rates of young kids; families moving out of poverty; and a significant impact on long-term outcomes of adults 19 years or older who attended Head Start.

The fact is Head Start does work for a vast majority of children. Can implementation of the program be improved? Of course. And it will be. Head Start has a 45-year history of continuous improvement. This study was conducted from 2002 to 2005. Two years ago, the Head Start reauthorization included many significant improvements to the program, some of which are in the process of taking effect and are not reflected in this study. This study likely will only catalyze the improvements already underway in Head Start since its reauthorization in late 2007.

We also need to improve the connections between the comprehensive services children receive in Head Start and the additional supports they may need to continue their successful progress in elementary schools. Head Start looks forward to working with the Department of Education and school districts across the country to help improve post–Head Start education by sharing strategies, such as parent involvement, that have worked well in Head Start and should work well in the elementary school setting.

> *"Head Start, the most sacrosanct federal education program,* doesn't work."

# Head Start Is a Failure

*Andrew J. Coulson*

*Andrew J. Coulson is the director of the Center for Educational Freedom at the Cato Institute. In the following viewpoint, he points to a 2010 study that shows that by the end of first grade, children who attended Head Start perform academically—and in other respects—at the same level as children who didn't. Coulson argues that this study proves that Head Start is a waste of money and effort. He suggests that President Obama and his fellow Democrats should end support for Head Start and instead support programs such as school choice, which have proven successful.*

As you read, consider the following questions:

1. How much has Head Start cost over its 45-year history, according to Coulson?

2. According to the author, how many of the 114 tests administered to first graders showed a significant advantage from participating in Head Start?

3. In 2009, to what level did President Obama raise the annual funding for Head Start?

Head Start, the most sacrosanct federal education program, *doesn't work.*

That's the finding of a sophisticated study just released by President [Barack] Obama's Department of Health and Human Services.

## What the Study Shows

Created in 1965, the comprehensive preschool program for 3- and 4-year-olds and their parents is meant to narrow the education gap between low-income students and their middle- and upper-income peers. Forty-five years and $166 billion later, it has been proven a failure.

The bad news came in the study released this month [January 2010]: It found that, by the end of the first grade, children who attended Head Start are essentially indistinguishable from a control group of students who didn't.

What's so damning is that this study used the best possible method to review the program: It looked at a nationally representative sample of 5,000 children who were randomly assigned to either the Head Start ("treatment") group or to the non–Head Start ("control") group.

Random assignment is the "gold standard" of medical and social-science research: It gives investigators confidence that the treatment and control groups are essentially identical in every respect except their access to Head Start. So if eventual test performances differ, we can be pretty sure that the difference was caused by the program. No previous study of Head Start used this approach on a nationally representative sample of children.

## Dramatic Results

When the researchers gave both groups of students 44 different academic tests at the end of the first grade, only two seemed to show even marginally significant advantages for the Head Start group. And even those apparent advantages vanished after standard statistical controls were applied.

In fact, not a single one of the *114* tests administered to first graders—of academics, socio-emotional development, health care/health status and parenting practice—showed a reliable, statistically significant effect from participating in Head Start.

Some advocates of the program have acknowledged these dramatic results, but suggest that it's not necessarily Head Start's fault if its effects vanish during kindergarten and the first grade—perhaps our K–12 schools are to blame.

But that's beside the point. Even if it's true, it means that Head Start will be of no lasting value to children until we fix our elementary and secondary schools. Until then, money spent on Head Start will continue to be wasted.

Yet the Obama administration remains enthusiastic. Health and Human Services Secretary Kathleen Sibelius and Education Secretary Arne Duncan both want to *boost* funding for Head Start—that is, to spend more on a program that's *sure to fail*. That's after the president already raised spending on the program from $6.8 billion to $9.2 billion last year [2009].

## The DC Opportunity Scholarship Program

Instead of throwing more dollars at this proven failure, President Obama might consider throwing his weight behind proven successes. A federal program that pays private-school tuition for poor [Washington,] DC families, for instance, has been shown to raise students' reading performance by more than two grade levels after just three years, compared to a control group of students who stayed in public schools. And it does so at about a quarter the cost to taxpayers of DC's public schools.

Sadly, Obama and Duncan have ignored the DC program's proven success. Neither lifted a finger to save it when Democrats in Congress pulled the plug on its funding last year.

Perhaps it's unrealistic to expect national Democrats to end a Great Society [a set of domestic programs initiated by President Lyndon B. Johnson] program, even when it's a proven failure. Perhaps it's unrealistic to expect them to stand up to teachers' union opposition and support private-school-choice programs that are proven successes.

Of course, until last week, it seemed unrealistic to expect a Republican to win the Senate seat long held by Ted Kennedy. If voters get angry enough with federal education politics, national Democrats may start learning from their state-level colleagues who *are* starting to support effective policies like school choice. Or *they* may just lose their seats, too.

> *"No Child Left Behind is one size fits all. But any experienced teacher knows how warped a yardstick that is."*

# No Child Left Behind Is Harmful and Should Not Be Funded

## Susan J. Hobart

*Susan Hobart is an elementary school teacher. In the following viewpoint, she asserts that No Child Left Behind fails students because it is a one-size-fits-all approach to students with diverse backgrounds and abilities. In addition, it forces teachers to "teach to the test," spending far too much time on test-taking strategies rather than learning. Hobart advocates an emphasis on the children, addressing their needs and not those of the testing companies.*

As you read, consider the following questions:

1. In what way does the author believe No Child Left Behind is part of a larger attack on public education?

2. What are the author's specific recommendations to improve academic achievement?

3. How does Hobart want to be remembered by her students in the coming years?

I'm a teacher. I've taught elementary school for eleven years. I've always told people, "I have the best job in the world." I crafted curriculum that made students think, and they had fun while learning. At the end of the day, I felt energized. Today, more often than not, I feel demoralized.

While I still connect my lesson plans to students' lives and work to make it real, this no longer is my sole focus. Today I have a new nickname: testbuster. Singing to the tune of "Ghostbusters," I teach test-taking strategies similar to those taught in Stanley Kaplan prep courses for the SAT. I spend an inordinate amount of time showing students how to "bubble up," the term for darkening those little circles that accompany multiple choice questions on standardized tests.

I am told these are invaluable skills to have.

I am told if we do a good job, our students will do well.

I am told that our district does not teach to the test.

I am told that the time we are spending preparing for and administering the tests, analyzing the results, and attending in-services to help our children become proficient on this annual measure of success will pay off by reducing the academic achievement gap between our white children and our children of color.

I am told a lot of things.

But what I know is that I'm not the teacher I used to be. And it takes a toll. I used to be the one who raved about my classroom, even after a long week. Pollyanna [a naive person], people called me. Today, when I speak with former colleagues, they are amazed at the cynicism creeping into my voice.

What has changed?

## The Effect of No Child Left Behind

No Child Left Behind is certainly a big part of the problem. The children I test are from a wide variety of abilities and backgrounds. Whether they have a cognitive disability, speak entry-level English, or have speech or language delays, everyone takes the same test and the results are posted. Special education students may have some accommodations, but they take the same test and are expected to perform at the same level as general education students. Students new to this country or with a native language other than English must also take the same test and are expected to perform at the same level as children whose native language is English. Picture yourself taking a five-day test in French after moving to Paris last year.

No Child Left Behind is one size fits all. But any experienced teacher knows how warped a yardstick that is.

I spent yesterday in a meeting discussing this year's [2008] standardized test results. Our team was feeling less than optimistic in spite of additional targeted funds made available to our students who are low income or who perform poorly on such tests.

As an educator, I know these tests are only one measure, one snapshot, of student achievement. Unfortunately, they are the make-or-break assessment that determines our status with the Department of Education.

They are the numbers that are published in the paper.

They are the scores that homebuyers look at when deciding if they should move into a neighborhood.

They are the numbers that are pulled out and held over us, as more and greater rigidity enters the curriculum.

I was recently told we cannot buddy up with a first-grade class during our core literacy time. It does not fit the definition of core literacy, I was told. Reading with younger children has been a boon to literacy improvement for my struggling readers and my new English-speaking students. Now I must throw this tool away?

## One-Size-Fits-All Approach Does Not Work

In an increasingly diverse public school setting, there is not one educational pedagogy that fits all students. We study and discuss differentiated curriculum, modify teaching strategies, and set "just right reading levels" to scaffold student learning. But No Child Left Behind doesn't care about that. It takes no note of where they started or how much they may have progressed.

As a teacher, I measure progress and achievement for my students on a daily basis. I set the bar high, expecting a lot.

I don't argue with the importance of assessment; it informs my instruction for each child.

I don't argue with the importance of accountability; I believe in it strongly—for myself and my students.

I have empathy for our administrators who have to stand up and be told that we are "challenged schools." And I have empathy for our administrators who have to turn around and drill it into our teacher heads, telling us we must do things "this" way to get results. I feel for them. They are judged on the numbers, as well.

## The Larger Issue

No Child Left Behind is a symptom of a larger problem: the attack on public education itself. Like the school choice effort, which uses public funds to finance private schools and cherry-pick the best students, No Child Left Behind is designed to punish public schools and to demonstrate that private is best.

But I don't think we've turned a corner that we can't come back from. Public education has been a dynamic vehicle in our country since its inception. We must grapple with maintaining this progressive institution. Policymakers and educators know that education holds out hope as the great equalizer in this country. It can inspire and propel a student, a family, a community.

## Why No Child Left Behind Is a Failure

After six years, there is overwhelming evidence that the deeply flawed "No Child Left Behind" law (NCLB) is doing more harm than good in our nation's public schools. NCLB's test-and-punish approach to school reform relies on limited, one-size-fits-all tools that reduce education to little more than test prep. It produces unfair decisions and requires unproven, often irrational "solutions" to complex problems. NCLB is clearly underfunded, but fully funding a bad law is not a solution.

*"'No Child Left Behind' After Six Years: An Escalating Trade Record of Failure,"* FairTest, *January 25, 2008.*

The state where I teach has a large academic achievement gap for African American and low income children. That is unacceptable. Spending time, money, energy on testing everyone with a "one size fits all test" will not eliminate or reduce that gap.

## What Needs to Be Done

Instead, we need teacher-led professional development and more local control of school budgets and policymaking. Beyond that, we need to address the economic and social issues many children face, instead of punishing the schools that are trying to do right by these students.

We've got things backwards today. Children should be in the front seat, not the testing companies. And teachers should be rewarded for teaching, not for being Stanley Kaplan tutors.

Ten years ago, I taught a student named Cayla. A couple of months ago, I got a note from her, one of those things that teachers thrive on.

"Ms. Hobart was different than other teachers, in a good way," she wrote. "We didn't learn just from a textbook; we experienced the topics by 'jumping into the textbook.' We got to construct a rainforest in our classroom, have a fancy lunch on the Queen Elizabeth II, and go on a safari through Africa. What I learned ten years ago still sticks with me today. When I become a teacher, I hope to inspire my students as much as she inspired hers."

## Another Success Story

Last week, I received a call from Niecy, another student from that class ten years ago. She was calling from southern Illinois to tell me she was graduating from high school this month and had just found out that she has won a scholarship to a college in Indiana. I was ecstatic in my happiness for her. We laughed, and I told her I was looking at a photo of her on my wall, building a pyramid out of paper bricks with her classmates.

I also had a recent conversation with Manuel in a grocery parking lot. He reminded me of my promise eight years ago to attend his high school graduation. I plan to be there.

Cayla and Niecy and Manuel are three of the reasons I teach. They are the reasons that some days this still feels like a passion and not a job.

When I pick up the broom at the end of the day to sweep my class due to budget cuts, I remember Cayla.

When I drive home demoralized after another meeting where our success is dissected with a knife manufactured in Texas, I remember Niecy.

When another new program that is going to solve the reading disparity, resulting in higher test scores, is introduced on top of another new program that was supposed to result in the same thing, I remember Manuel.

They are the fires that fuel my passion. They are the lifeboats that help me ride this current wave in education.

Eight or ten years from now, I want other former students to contact me and tell me a success story from their lives. I don't want to be remembered as the teacher who taught them how to sing "Testbusters" or to "bubble up." I want to be remembered as a teacher who inspired them to learn.

| "The way forward starts with a more realistic assessment of what the federal government can reasonably hope to achieve in education."

# No Child Left Behind Should Be Reformed

## Michael J. Petrilli

*Michael J. Petrilli is the vice president of the Thomas B. Fordham Foundation and a research fellow at the Hoover Institution. In the following viewpoint, he admits that he has come to the conclusion that No Child Left Behind is fundamentally flawed, but that its ideals are so important that it should be reformed rather than repealed. Petrilli recommends a series of key reforms that depend on educators and legislators recognizing the limitations of the federal government and turning over important provisions of the law to state governments, which are better suited to be successful in educational reform.*

As you read, consider the following questions:

1. What does Petrilli consider flawed about No Child Left Behind's incentives to boost achievement in reading and math?

2. What are the two responsibilities the author believes the federal government should assume under a revised No Child Left Behind?

3. What are two responsibilities that the author thinks would be better suited to state governments under a revised No Child Left Behind?

For five years now [since 2002], I've considered myself a supporter of the No Child Left Behind Act [NCLB]. And not just the casual flag-waver variety. Much of that time I spent inside the [George W.] Bush administration, trying to make the law work, explaining its vision to hundreds of audiences, even wearing an NCLB pin on my lapel. I was a True Believer.

## Supporting the Ideals Behind NCLB

In a way, I still am. After all, in the 21st century, saying you "support" NCLB is shorthand for affirming a set of ideas, values, and hopes for the country as much as an expression about a particular statute. I'm not just referring to the proposition that "no child should be left behind"—the notion that we have a moral responsibility to provide a decent education for everyone. Ninety-nine percent of the education establishment can get behind that "purpose" of the law and still resist meaningful reform.

I mean a set of powerful—and controversial—ideas that provide the subtext for all the big NCLB battles. First, that virtually all children (even those living in poverty) have the capacity to achieve a reasonable level of proficiency in reading and math by the time they turn 18—and that it's the education system's job to make sure they do. Second, that everyone benefits from having someone looking over his shoulder and that schools and school systems need external pressure—i.e., accountability—in order to improve; good intentions aren't enough. Third, that good education is synonymous with good teaching. This requires good teachers, which every child deserves, but which today's education bureaucracies, licensure rules, ed schools, and union contracts too often impede. Fourth, that giving parents choices within the education system has all kinds of positive benefits, from creating healthy competitive pressures to allowing educators to customize their programs instead of trying to be all things to all people. And fifth, that improving education is a national imperative, and that the federal government can and should play a constructive role.

## NCLB Is Fundamentally Flawed

In other words, at the level of ideas, NCLB is the embodiment of the 1990s-era education reform playbook. Educators, policymakers, think tankers, and activists who "support" NCLB are saying "I'm part of the education reform team."

But does that mean that they necessarily agree with the machinery of the law itself? Speaking personally, I've gradually and reluctantly come to the conclusion that NCLB as enacted is fundamentally flawed and probably beyond repair.

Of course, I harbored doubts about certain specifics from the beginning. You didn't have to be a genius to see to see the "highly qualified teachers" mandate as a huge overreach and a probable failure, as it took a reasonable notion (teachers should know their stuff) and tried to enforce it through a rigid rule-based mechanism (second-guessing principals who, for instance, hired engineers as math teachers). Nor was it hard to determine that asking all states to reach universal "proficiency" by 2014 but allowing them to define "proficiency" as they saw fit would create a race to the bottom.

## Other Flaws

Other flaws took me longer to appreciate. For example:

- Surely schools would respond thoughtfully to the law's incentives to boost achievement in reading and math, and would understand that providing a broad, content-rich education would give them the best shot at boosting test scores, right? Yet the anecdotes (and increasingly, evidence) keep rolling in of schools turning into test-prep factories and narrowing the curriculum.

- Surely if those of us at the Department of Education pushed hard enough we could get districts to inform parents of their school-choice options under the law, and ensure that kids trapped in failing schools have better places to go, right? Yet . . . hard experience has shown that "stronger implementation" would only make a difference at the margin. It cannot solve the fundamental problem: in most of our big cities, there are too few good schools to go around. Uncle Sam can't snap his fingers and make it otherwise. Furthermore, while it's hard enough to force recalcitrant states and districts to do things they don't want to do, it's impossible to force them to do those things well. And when it comes to informing parents, creating new schools, or implementing almost any of NCLB's many pieces, it's not enough for states or districts to go through the motions. They have to *want* to make it succeed. If they don't, Washington is out of luck. It has no tools or levers to alter the situation. That's why I've called much of the law "un-implementable."

So I shouldn't have been surprised when the AFT's [American Federation of Teachers] Michele McLauglin wrote in her NCLB blog about the AEI [American Enterprise Institute] conference, "Petrilli and Checker Finn . . . seem to be arguing for a more limited role for the feds in education because the U.S. Department of Education doesn't have the ability to get states and districts to implement the law well. Unless I am missing something, this seems to be a shift in position for the Fordham Foundation, which has been a major supporter of NCLB."

## Facing Reality on NCLB

Guilty as charged. I can't pretend any longer that the law is "working," or that a tweak and a tuck would make it "work." Yet I still like its zeitgeist [spirit]. As Kati Haycock argued at the AEI confab, NCLB has "changed the conversation" in education. Results are now the coin of the realm; the "soft bigotry of low expectations" is taboo; closing the achievement gap is at the top of everyone's to-do list. All for the good. More than good. But let's face it: it doesn't help the dedicated principal who is pulling her hair out because of the law's nonsensical provisions—the specifics that keep NCLB from achieving its own aims.

Here's the crux of the matter: when it's time for reauthorization, can we overhaul the law itself without letting go of its powerful ideas? Two other outcomes are more likely. One is the tweak regimen: the law gets renewed but remains mostly unchanged, and we continue to muddle through, driving even well-intentioned educators crazy and not achieving the results we seek. (This is the prediction of most "education insiders." It amounts to ostrich-like stubbornness in the face of evidence that an overhaul is what's needed.) The second is bathtub emptying: Throw the baby out along with the murky water and give up on the law *and* its ideals. Then we go back to the days when schools felt little pressure to get all of their students prepared for college and life and democratic participation, and we declare No Child Left Behind another failed experiment.

That would be a disaster.

What, then, to do? In my opinion, the way forward starts with a more realistic assessment of what the federal government can reasonably hope to achieve in education. Using sticks and carrots to tug and prod states and districts in desired directions has proven unworkable. It was worth trying but experience has taught us that this approach suffers from too much hubris and humility at the same time. Instead of this muddle, the feds should adopt a simple, radical principle: Do it yourself, or don't do it at all.

## "Do It Yourself" Reforms

In the "Do it Yourself" category would be two major responsibilities: distributing funds to the neediest students, and collecting and publishing transparent information about the performance of U.S. schools. Redistributing funds is easy; it's what Washington [D.C., i.e., the federal government] does best. Still, it could do it even better by adopting weighted-student funding, ensuring that dollars follow children to their school of choice, with extra cash following students with the greatest needs. Furthermore, it could do more to ensure that high-poverty schools receive equitable resources before the federal dollars arrive. . . .

As for its second responsibility, an important bullet waits to be bitten: collect and publish swift, reliable, and comparable data on the performance of the nation's schools via clear national standards, a rigorous national test, and a common approach to school ratings (e.g., a single definition of "adequate yearly progress"). Then everyone would have a consistent and fair way to distinguish good schools from bad. We would have consistently high expectations for all students and all schools, and would end the federal/state cat-and-mouse games being played over accountability. The federal government should also make school-level financial information transparent (a necessity to achieve the funding reforms mentioned above) and continue to pay for high-quality research and make its results transparent and accessible to all.

## "Don't-Do-It-At-All" Reforms

Into the "Don't Do It At All" bucket goes everything else. No more federal mandates on teacher quality. No more prescriptive "cascade of sanctions" for failing schools. No more federal guarantee of school choice for children not being well-served.

# Reforms of No Child Left Behind

Reforming our schools to deliver a world-class education is a shared responsibility—the task cannot be shouldered by our nation's teachers and principals alone. We must foster school environments where teachers have the time to collaborate, the opportunities to lead, and the respect that all professionals deserve. . . . We must support families, communities, and schools working in partnership to deliver services and supports that address the full range of student needs.

This effort will also require our best thinking and resources—to support innovative approaches to teaching and learning; to bring lasting change to our lowest-performing schools; and to investigate and evaluate what works and what can work better in America's schools. Instead of labeling failures, we will reward success. Instead of a single snapshot, we will recognize progress and growth. And instead of investing in the status quo, we must reform our schools to accelerate student achievement, close achievement gaps, inspire our children to excel, and turn around those schools that for too many young Americans aren't providing them with the education they need to succeed in college and a career.

My Administration's blueprint for reauthorization of the Elementary and Secondary Education Act is not only a plan to renovate a flawed law, but also an outline for a re-envisioned federal role in education. This is a framework to guide our deliberations and shared work . . . to strengthen America's public education system.

*Barack Obama, "Blueprint for Reform,"*
*US Department of Education, March 2010.*

The states would worry about how to define and achieve greater teacher quality (or, better, teacher effectiveness). The states would decide when and how to intervene in failing schools. The states would develop new capacity for school choice. These are all important, powerful reforms, but they have proven beyond Uncle Sam's capacity to make happen. These policy battles should return to the state level, where governments can actually do something about them and do them right. And if the federal government just can't help itself and wants to "promote" these causes, let it offer competitive grants for states and districts that want to move in these directions.

The Do It Yourself or Don't Do It At All Act doesn't have the same ring as leaving no child behind. But its zeitgeist is the same. It would also be a better fit for our federalist system and a more effective vehicle for the reform ideas that we NCLB supporters hold so dear. In this new year, let us resolve to be humble enough to admit the law's limitations and brave enough to stand up for its ideals.

# Periodical and Internet Sources Bibliography

*The following articles have been selected to supplement the diverse views presented in this chapter.*

| | |
|---|---|
| Lindsey Burke and David Muhlhausen | "Head Start Doesn't Work," The Heritage Foundation, May 31, 2010. |
| Conn Carroll | "Choice for the Powerful, Not for the People," *The Bulletin*, March 31, 2010. |
| Edwin Feulner | "'Let Me Rise': School Choice in DC," The Heritage Foundation, January 13, 2010. |
| Kelly E. Flynn | "No Child Left Behind Act Has a Dirty Little Secret; It's Called Segregation," *Flint Journal*, February 15, 2009. |
| Gregory Kane | "Charter Schools Don't Work? Results Say Differently," *Washington Examiner*, June 21, 2010. |
| Linda Kulman | "Reform of 'No Child Left Behind' Calls for More Flexibility, Higher Standards," *Politics Daily*, March 17, 2010. |
| Charles Murray | "Why Charter Schools Fail the Test," *New York Times*, May 5, 2010. |
| Diane Ravitch | "The Big Idea—It's Bad Education Policy," *New York Times*, March 13, 2010. |
| *USA Today* | "Our View on Early Education: Fix Head Start Before Throwing More Money at It," July 12, 2010. |
| Marcus Winters | "City Charter Schools Aren't Just Better—They Cost Less," *New York Daily News*, March 1, 2010. |

# For Further Discussion

## Chapter 1

1. Are school funds being spent effectively? Read viewpoints from Marcus A. Winters and Arne Duncan to inform your opinion.

2. In his viewpoint, Jason Reece maintains that school funding is always affected during economic downturns. Arthur Peng and James Guthrie, however, point out that the federal government steps in to fill funding gaps during tough economic times. Whose argument do you find more convincing and why?

3. After reading viewpoints by Lynne K. Varner and *The Daily Collegian*, offer your opinion on whether federal stimulus funds should be used to fund education. Use information from the viewpoints to support your position.

## Chapter 2

1. Are weighted student funding formulas a fair and effective way to fund education? Christian Braunlich believes they are a just way to allocate resources. Nicole Gelinas, however, does not. Use information from the viewpoints to support your opinion on the funding strategy.

2. In the mid-2000s, the 65 Percent Solution was considered an important innovation in school funding reform. Read viewpoints by George F. Will and Susan Phillips. Do you think more school districts should have adopted the strategy? Why or why not?

3. Kevin D. Teasley contends that the Race to the Top program has resulted in education reforms. Frederick M. Hess counters by arguing that the reforms implemented under

the program are not the ones truly needed in education today. Which argument do you find more compelling in light of the information provided in each viewpoint?

## Chapter 3

1. School choice has been a controversial topic in education for the past several years. Marcus A. Winters maintains that vouchers are a great way to improve academic achievement and offer a quality education for more students. In a countering viewpoint, Greg Anrig points out that school vouchers have not improved education. Read both viewpoints to inform your opinion. Do you think school vouchers are a beneficial educational strategy? Why or why not?

2. In his viewpoint, Ron Wolk contends that charter schools are a wise investment of public money. William G. Wraga, however, argues that charter schools have not been an improvement over traditional public schools. After reading both viewpoints, do you think charter schools are worth the investment?

3. The termination of the D.C. Opportunity Scholarship program generated an uproar in certain education circles. After reading viewpoints written by Alex Koppelman and published by Targeted News Service, give your opinion on the issue. Was it ultimately a beneficial program for Washington, D.C., schoolchildren? Should it be revived?

4. Are magnet schools a prudent investment of public money? Susan Eaton asserts that they are. Victor Harbison believes that they are fundamentally flawed and have been bad for education. Which perspective do you agree with and why?

5. The effectiveness of No Child Left Behind has been a popular topic in politics and education. In the last two viewpoints of the chapter, the fate of the program is discussed: Susan J. Hobart deems it a failure and argues that

it should be abandoned, and Michael J. Petrilli suggests significant reform. What is your assessment of No Child Left Behind? Should the government have continued to fund it as is, reformed it, or repealed it? Use the viewpoints to inform your answer.

# Organizations to Contact

*The editors have compiled the following list of organizations concerned with the issues debated in this book. The descriptions are derived from materials provided by the organizations. All have publications or information available for interested readers. The list was compiled on the date of publication of the present volume; names, addresses, phone and fax numbers, and e-mail and Internet addresses may change. Be aware that many organizations take several weeks or longer to respond to inquiries, so allow as much time as possible.*

**Achieve**
1775 Eye Street NW, Suite 410, Washington, DC   20006
(202) 419-1540 • fax: (202) 828-0911
website: www.achieve.org

Achieve is an independent, nonpartisan organization focused on passing effective and meaningful educational reform, such as raising academic standards and strengthening accountability. In 2005 it launched the American Diploma Project Network, which brings together business executives, school officials, and politicians to align high school standards and assessment and accountability systems. The organization's annual report, *Closing the Expectations Gap*, monitors states' progress in reaching these goals. Achieve also conducts extensive research and publishes state and national reports as well as policy briefs. It also publishes a monthly e-newsletter, *Perspective*, which focuses on current issues and provides updates on recent initiatives.

**American Association of School Administrators (AASA)**
801 N. Quincy Street, Suite 700, Arlington, VA   22203
(703) 528-0700 • fax: (703) 841-1543
e-mail: info@aasa.org
website: www.aasa.org

Established in 1865, the American Association of School Administrators (AASA) is a professional organization composed of more than thirteen thousand school officials, including superintendents, chief executive officers, and school administrators. The AASA works to develop school leaders and support effective educational policies that benefit students. AASA also acts as an advocate for students and children's causes. One of the issues it is currently involved in is childhood obesity; the organization publishes a monthly e-newsletter, *Healthy Learning News*, which disseminates various initiatives around the country focused on healthy eating. AASA also publishes the *School Administrator*, the organization's monthly magazine featuring articles on education, leadership, and issues that affect students and administrators.

## American Educational Research Association (AERA)

1430 K Street NW, Suite 1200, Washington, DC 20005
(202) 238-3200 • fax: (202) 238-3250
website: www.aera.net

The American Educational Research Association (AERA) is an international professional organization concerned with advancing educational research to reform teaching and testing policies with the ultimate goal being an efficient and effective education system. AERA seeks not only to advance knowledge about education, but also to apply that research in effective ways. AERA publishes a number of research studies and handbooks, all of which are available at its online bookstore. In addition, it offers several journals that provide in-depth research and analysis, including *American Educational Research Journal, Educational Researcher, Review of Educational Research*, and *Educational Evaluation and Policy Analysis*.

## American Federation of Teachers (AFT)

555 New Jersey Ave. NW, Washington, DC 20001
(202) 879-4400
website: www.aft.org

Founded in 1916, the American Federation of Teachers (AFT) is a labor union representing more than 1.5 million teachers and school personnel, such as school librarians and cafeteria workers. One of its main responsibilities is to lobby politicians and other policy makers for educational policy reform. The AFT publishes the *American Teacher*, a bimonthly magazine that profiles successful and innovative teachers and schools as well as current news and policies that affect education. Other AFT publications include *American Educator, AFT on Campus, PSRP Reporter, Healthwire,* and *Public Employee Advocate.*

## Education Commission of the States (ECS)

700 Broadway, #810, Denver, CO   80203
(303) 299-3600 • fax: (303) 296-8332
e-mail: ecs@ecs.org
website: www.ecs.org

The Education Commission of the States (ECS) is a nonprofit, independent organization dedicated to improving education by "facilitating the exchange of information, ideas and experiences among state policy makers and education leaders." ECS works to build partnerships, share information, and advance effective and beneficial educational strategies. It publishes a quarterly magazine, *The Progress of Education Reform*, which explores current topics of interest in the education community. ECS also publishes a number of e-newsletters, including *ECS e-Connection, Citizenship Matters,* and *ECS e-Clips.* These publications can be accessed on the ECS website.

## Institute for Educational Leadership (IEL)

4455 Connecticut Ave. NW, Suite 310, Washington, DC   20008
(202) 822-8405 • fax: (202) 872-4050
e-mail: iel@iel.org
website: www.iel.org

The Institute for Educational Leadership (IEL) is a nonpartisan, nonprofit organization that works to strengthen the leadership capability of education professionals; build productive ties between schools, parents, and communities; and improve educational policies on the state and local levels. IEL publishes studies, handbooks, and research papers on educational reform and policy issues, including *Thinking and Learning About Leader and Leadership Development, Community Schools Across the Nation: A Sampling of Local Initiatives and National Models*, and *Guideposts for Success*. It also publishes the keynote lecture of its annual Danzberger Lecture Series, the archives of which are available on the organization's website.

### National Education Association (NEA)
1201 16th Street NW, Washington, DC   20036
(202) 833-4000 • fax: (202) 822-7974
website: www.nea.org

Founded in 1857, the National Education Association (NEA) is the largest labor union in the United States. The NEA represents more than 3.2 million public school teachers, school employees, college instructors and staff members, and retired educators. The association's mission is "to advocate for education professionals and to unite our members and the nation to fulfill the promise of public education to prepare every student to succeed in a diverse and interdependent world." The NEA's activities range from raising money for scholarship programs to developing training and leadership programs for teachers to lobbying for appropriate levels of school funding from local, state, and federal governments. The NEA Today is a website that offers the latest stories on education topics, as well as access to the *NEA Today* magazine. The NEA also publishes *Thought & Action*, a journal focused on education theory; *Tomorrow's Teachers*, a resource for teachers; and *Higher Education Advocate*, a bimonthly newsletter that explores issues important in higher education.

### National Head Start Association (NHSA)
1651 Prince Street, Alexandria, VA   22314
(703) 739-0875 • fax: (703) 739-0878
website: www.nhsa.org

The National Head Start Association (NHSA) is a nonprofit organization that advocates for the needs of students and families enrolled in the Head Start program. The NHSA lobbies for resources and government policies that will support Head Start and offers extensive training programs and professional development opportunities for Head Start instructors and staff. The NHSA also conducts research on the efficacy of Head Start and looks for ways to make it more effective. The organization's website features NHSA radio, which offers answers and advice for parents and administrators. It publishes *NHSA Dialog*, a peer-reviewed journal that analyzes the latest research on Head Start. The website also has an events calendar, which lists all upcoming training and professional events related to Head Start.

### National Parent Teacher Association (PTA)

1250 N. Pitt Street, Alexandria, VA  22314
(703) 518-1200 • fax: (703) 836-0942
e-mail: info@pta.org
website: www.pta.org

The National Parent Teacher Association (PTA) is the largest volunteer child advocacy organization in the United States. The PTA works with federal agencies and other national education, health, safety, and child advocacy groups to develop programs and policies that will benefit students and their parents. The PTA website hosts a bulletin board where PTA leaders and members can share ideas, a blog in which PTA officials can discuss current issues and upcoming events and access photos, videos, and podcasts. Also available on the website is PTA's online magazine, *Our Children*, which focuses on the concerns of parents of schoolchildren.

### National School Boards Association (NSBA)

1680 Duke Street, Alexandria, VA  22314
(703) 838-6722 • fax: (703) 683-7590
e-mail: info@nsba.org
website: www.nsba.org

The National School Boards Association (NSBA) is a nonprofit organization that represents state associations of school boards and their member districts in working relationships with the federal government and state agencies. The NSBA "supports the capacity of each school board, acting on behalf of and in close concert with the people of its community, to establish a structure and environment that allow all students to reach their maximum potential, to provide accountability to the community on performance in the schools, and to serve as the key community advocate for children and youth and their public schools." On the NSBA website there is a link to *School Board News Today*, which features recent stories and analysis on education issues. There is also a link to *American School Board Journal*, which offers stories and advice on school governance and student achievement.

## Public Education Network (PEN)

601 Thirteenth Street NW, Suite 710 South
Washington, DC   20005
(202) 628-3808
e-mail: pen@publiceducation.org
website: www.publiceducation.org

The Public Education Network (PEN) is an independent, national association of local education funds (community-backed educational reform organizations) and individuals working together to advance effective public school reform with the mission of improving public education in low-income communities. One of the organization's key tasks is to disseminate information about innovative school reform and quality educational programs around the country. To accomplish this, PEN publishes policy briefs, fact sheets, research papers, in-depth studies, and reports on subjects such as No Child Left Behind, teacher resources, and new funding initiatives and strategies. It also publishes a weekly e-newsletter found on its website, the PEN *Newsblast*, which features op-eds, press releases, and research on relevant school funding issues.

## US Department of Education

400 Maryland Ave. SW, Washington, DC    20202
(800) 872-5327
website: www.ed.gov

The US Department of Education is the federal department that establishes federal school funding policies, distributes funds, monitors school performance, and enforces federal law on discrimination in education. It also distributes financial aid to eligible students and oversees research on US schools in order to determine the success of educational programs across the country. After careful expert analysis of data, the department then makes well-considered recommendations for school reform. There are a range of publications available on the department's website, including handbooks, research papers, speeches, congressional testimony, and in-depth studies on reform and funding topics. It also publishes a number of journals and newsletters, including *Education Research News, ED-Info*, and *Education Innovator*.

# Bibliography of Books

Scott Franklin Abernathy
*School Choice and the Future of Democracy.* Ann Arbor: University of Michigan Press, 2005.

Susan L. Aud and Leon Michos
*Spreading Freedom and Saving Money: The Fiscal Impact of the D.C. Voucher Program.* Washington, DC: Cato Institute, 2006.

Mark Berends, Matthew G. Springer, Herbert J. Walberg, eds.
*Charter School Outcomes.* New York: Erlbaum, 2008.

Julian R. Betts et al.
*Does School Choice Work? Effects on Student Integration and Achievement.* San Francisco: Public Policy Institute of California, 2006.

Elizabeth Blake
*No Child Left Behind?: The True Story of a Teacher's Quest.* Poughkeepsie, NY: Hudson House, 2008.

Patricia Burch
*Hidden Markets: The New Education Privatization.* New York: Routledge, 2009.

Brian J. Caldwell and Jim M. Spinks
*Raising the Stakes: From Improvement to Transformation in the Reform of Schools.* New York: Routledge, 2008.

Ronald G. Corwin and E. Joseph Schneider
*The School Choice Hoax: Fixing America's Schools.* Lanham, MD: Rowman & Littlefield, 2007.

W. Norton Grubb  *The Money Myth: School Resources, Outcomes, and Equity.* New York: Russell Sage Foundation, 2009.

William Hayes  *No Child Left Behind: Past, Present, and Future.* Lanham, MD: Rowman & Littlefield, 2008.

Jeffrey R. Henig  *Spin Cycle: How Research Is Used in Policy Debates: The Case of Charter Schools.* New York: Russell Sage Foundation, 2008.

Frederick M. Hess  *Tough Love for Schools: Essays on Competition, Accountability, and Excellence.* Washington, DC: AEI Press, 2006.

Eugene G. Hickok  *Schoolhouse of Cards: An Inside Story of No Child Left Behind and Why America Needs a Real Education Revolution.* Lanham, MD: Rowman & Littlefield, 2010.

Paul T. Hill, ed.  *Charter Schools Against the Odds.* Stanford, CA: Education Next Books, 2006.

Richard G. Howell and Paul E. Peterson  *The Education Gap: Vouchers and Urban Schools.* Rev. ed. Washington, DC: Brookings Institution Press, 2006.

E. Jane Irons and Sandra Harris  *The Challenges of No Child Left Behind: Understanding the Issues of Excellence, Accountability, and Choice.* Lanham, MD: Rowman & Littlefield, 2007.

Richard D.
Kahlenberg, ed.

*Improving On No Child Left Behind: Getting Education Reform Back on Track.* New York: Century Foundation Press, 2008.

Helen F. Ladd
and Edward B.
Fiske, eds.

*Handbook of Research in Education Finance and Policy.* New York: Routledge, 2008.

Richard P.
McAdams

*Exploring the Myths and Realities of Today's Schools: A Candid Review of Challenges Educators Face.* Lanham, MD: Rowman & Littlefield, 2010.

Paul E. Peterson,
ed.

*Choice and Competition in American Education.* Lanham, MD: Rowman & Littlefield, 2006.

Jeanne M. Powers

*Charter Schools: From Reform Imagery to Reform Reality.* New York: Palgrave Macmillan, 2009.

Paul A. Sracic

*San Antonio v. Rodriguez and the Pursuit of Equal Education: The Debate over Discrimination and School Funding.* Lawrence: University Press of Kansas, 2006.

Brian M. Stecher
and Georges
Vernez

*Reauthorizing No Child Left Behind: Facts and Recommendations.* Santa Monica, CA: Rand Corp., 2010.

Gail L.
Sunderman, ed.

*Holding NCLB Accountable: Achieving Accountability, Equity and School Reform.* Thousand Oaks, CA: Corwin Press, 2008.

Geoffrey Walford

*Markets and Equity in Education.* New York: Continuum, 2006.

# Index